Sick Kids
And Those Who
Love Them

Karen Rhea

Copyright © 2003 by Karen Rhea

Sick Kids And Those Who Love Them
by Karen Rhea

Printed in the United States of America

ISBN 1-594670-10-2

All rights reserved. No part of this publication may be reproduced or transmitted in any form or by any means without written permission of the author.

Scripture taken from the HOLY BIBLE, NEW INTERNATIONAL VERSION, Copyright © 1973, 1978, 1984 by International Bible Society. Used by permission of Zondervan Publishing House. All rights reserved.

The "NIV" and "New International Version" trademarks are registered in the United States Patent and Trademark Office by International Bible Society. Use of either trademark requires the permission of International Bible Society.

Names and identities of some of the persons have been changed in order to protect their privacy.

Contributed stories; Ginger Gibson, Jan Maloney and Jim Maloney

Xulon Press
www.XulonPress.com

Xulon Press books are available in bookstores everywhere, and on the Web at www.XulonPress.com.

Acknowledgments

Thank you to the parents who shared their personal stories with me. Your honesty will surely help others glean knowledge and hope from your precious children's lives.

How do I express a thankful heart following a season of sorrow? With time, the realization surfaced that giving thanks to my Savior, Jesus of Nazareth, before any evidence of a blessing would be the beginning of joy.

Hats off.......
- To my boy, William Joel Rhea, whose very being brought a completeness to my world.
- To my husband, Jim Rhea, whose integrity, affection and humor provide me with the knowledge that he will always be the love of my life.
- To my parents, Bill and Gwen Du Bois, who provided me with sweet memories and lots of material!
- The Rhea and Heldebrand clans; family one and all.
- Jimmy, Lara, Alan, Jakob and Erik for allowing me to belong and feel so loved.
- To my nephew, Michael, whose tender heart and fine achievements provide a glimpse into the culmination

of his mother's dreams.
- To my sister, Sue, whose twenty nine years on this earth helped me to expectantly anticipate eternity.
- To Susan, Dee and Mom for your generosity in proofreading this manuscript.
- To Sherrie Biernacki for your friendship, teaching and editing.
- To Sean, for catching the vision of Shar's and my dream. You are a true web artist.
- To Rick, Shar and Travis, who visited faithfully.
- To Bill's faithful friend, Sarah.
- To the women at Community Bible Study.
- To our friends in Poolesville, David and Susan, Frank and Carolyn, Rick and Peg.
- To our faithful friends at Boyds Presbyterian Church; Merritt, Debbie, Dick and Cory.
- To all the pastors, their wives, Billy's youth group, (thank you Drew) at the Church of the Redeemer in Gaithersburg, MD.
- To Steve & Wendy and Pat & Jennifer.
- To Boy Scout Troop 496 in Poolesville, Maryland, the Scout leaders and all the parents.
- To Bill's outstanding teachers.
- To Monica Buhl, for being Bill's first driving instructor.
- To my oldest friends, who are like family, Eric and Kris, Gail, Debby, Diane and Mary.
- Thank you David *Lyndsay* Rouse. You showed maturity beyond your years.
- To Mehrnoosh, who held Billy through the night until we arrived.
- To the medical community who tried their best and admitted that it was not enough.
- Thank you, Dr. Gail Transeau. Your expertise and compassion has helped to guide Bill to the young man

God intends for him to be.
- To the teachers and administration at Northwest High School in Germantown, MD. To Mrs. Gipe & Mr. O; you both encouraged music to come alive in Bill's heart once again.
- Jim and Bill, I love you guys. For your willingness to relive all the painful memories, as you read, corrected, reread and listened endlessly to our very personal stories unfold.

I Dedicate This Book To Parents Who Have...

- received another call from the school nurse.
- returned from another conference at their child's school due to absences from illness.
- cancelled another social engagement to be home with their sick child.
- helplessly watched as your baby was whisked away to the neonatal ICU.
- listened as their child cries in pain with an earache in the middle of the night.
- spilled liquid antibiotics all over their screaming baby.
- held their feverish child in a cool bath tub and watched them shiver.
- held down their child as they got shots or sutures.
- kept a medicine cabinet that resembles a pharmacy.
- felt their second home is the pediatrician's office and their third home is the specialist.
- no memory of why they ever got married.
- longed to be loved and understood and are just plain exhausted.
- just paid their monthly bill for their health insurance premiums.
- just paid their monthly bills to the hospital, radiologist, pediatrician and lab.

- slept in a fold-out chair in their child's hospital room.
- anxiously awaited news in the recovery room.
- been stunned and grieved at a ghastly diagnosis
- had to tell their child that further treatment is needed.
- pondered who will care for their adult child when they die.
- crumbled in grief by the casket of their precious child.
- continued to pay the medical bills for years after their child has died.
- AND To every doctor, nurse and technician that cares for our kids and loves their work.

Preface

Caring for our sick children opens a door to a private club that no one would choose to attend. We witness the playful innocence of our children stolen away. Their social lives and academics often suffer. Weary parents have no time and few resources for encouragement and direction. Frequent leave from work to care for chronically ill children adds to job loss and stress in the family. Financial problems and inability to communicate often result in fractured marriages.

When our kids are ill, that becomes our primary focus. The most needy ones require nothing less than our undivided, tender care. Unfortunately, others we love get lost by the wayside. It's simply too painful and embarrassing to share the deteriorations that occur in the privacy of our homes.

Our club needs some new rules. If your marriage is still intact, nurture it. Remember often the best part of the two of you. Acknowledge how you each grieve your child's illness differently. Talk to a friend who won't condemn your spouse. If you have a pediatrician you like, count your blessings. If not, find a new one. You and your child deserve nothing less. A community of faith is a necessary support system.

Finally, pray as a family. If you don't currently do this, a comfortable starting place is in the dark, around your child's bed at night. Parents of sick kids usually end up there anyway. Place your hands on your child and simply ask God for His healing touch on your precious child for that day. Thank Him for this life and pour out your cares on Him. Be faithful in asking the Lord into your home. He is waiting for an invitation.

BOOK I

A Season of Advocacy

Table of Contents

Chapter 1	Is Anybody Listening?	15
Chapter 2	Reflection	21
Chapter 3	Resignation	29
Chapter 4	Poor Judgment	35
Chapter 5	Provision	45
Chapter 6	Absentee Compassion	53
Chapter 7	A Dad's Dedication	61
Chapter 8	Music Silenced	67
Chapter 9	Hindering Help	75
Chapter 10	What Childhood?	83
Chapter 11	A Marriage in Crisis	89
Chapter 12	Friendship	99
Chapter 13	Achievements	107
Chapter 14	Am I Dying?	113
Chapter 15	Blinded Men	119
Chapter 16	Deception Versus Light	123
Chapter 17	Preparation	131
Chapter 18	Anticipation	137
Chapter 19	Servants of God	143
Chapter 20	Called To This Very Moment	149
Chapter 21	Trust Abandoned	153
Chapter 22	Revenge to Restoration	159
Chapter 23	Settling In	165
Chapter 24	A Season of Adjusting	171

Chapter 1

Is Anybody Listening?

Chapter 1

"Is Anybody Listening?"

By: Karen Rhea

I've never felt so alone. Are You there, God? Do You love my child as much as I do?

> **Isaiah 43; 2-3**
> *When you pass through the waters, I will be with you; and when you pass through the rivers, they will not sweep over you. When you walk through the fire, you will not be burned; the flames will not set you ablaze. For I am the Lord, your God, the Holy One of Israel, your Savior.*

I sat by my son's bedside in the intensive care unit. Glancing at the clock, I saw it was 3:00 a.m. The date was March 4, 2000. Earlier that afternoon, while home alone, Billy had called his best friend, David Lyndsay Rouse. As they talked, my son lost all feeling in his extremities. "Help me," was the last thing he said. Noticing his friend's speech was terribly slurred, Lyndsay, as he was better known, quickly called 911. In the ambulance, Billy's ability to answer simple questions deteriorated. Once he arrived in the emergency room, he became confused and disoriented. Screaming and thrashing, he broke out of his restraints. After four hours of being combative, our sixteen-year old son fell into unconsciousness.

He was slipping away, yet no one knew what was wrong. My husband, Jim, and I were not surprised because the doctors had been baffled for six long years. We had been instructed by several physicians to seek psychological help for Billy, as his health continued to spiral toward his present critical condition . Now, a doctor tried to prepare us for the inevitable. There was one remote possibility being researched, but the only words that filled my mind were: "Your son may not live through the night."

I cried out to God, "Please don't let him die, Lord. Send someone, anyone who will tell us what is wrong." It was the same prayer I had repeated for so many years. But never with such horror and intense sorrow. Jim stepped out of the room to get his composure.

With every rhythmic beep of Billy's heart monitor, I could hear my own heart pound. I realized I was breathing in and out in unison with my son. As I positioned myself on his hospital bed, I touched his hand, carefully avoiding the IV entering a tiny vein below his wrist. My own veins pulsed with grief and anger, as if those emotions were demanding the two of us to stay alive. I felt nothing else.

A nurse came into the room every ten minutes. I acknowledged her once with a nod. Engaging in casual conversation was useless. The sound of my own voice was strangely muffled and ugly. If repeating Billy's medical history would have changed the nightmare, I would have shouted it from the rooftop. But it was no use. I simply stared at my Billy in total disbelief.

Finally, it was dawn. I realized I needed to get my toothbrush out of the car. Pulling myself upright, I exchanged weary glances with Jim as I moved away from my boy. Taking my place on the bed, Jim kissed Billy's forehead and lingered there as his own tears wet Billy's ashen face, creating a horrible snapshot in my mind. The only way to close the shutter was to turn and leave. Exiting the room, I headed to my car to retrieve my overnight bag. Yet my energy was gone. What if something unspeakable happened while I was away from him? With each step I felt a weight of reluctance in leaving Billy's side.

As I left the warmth of the hospital, the cold night air hit me in the face. Spotting our car, I quickened my stride and became aware of a strange noise nearby. Was someone choking? Fumbling with my car keys, I realized the sound was my own sobs. I hopped into the car, turned on the ignition and blasted the heat. I sat in the warmth, recalling the events that brought Billy to this day. It began when he was ten years old.

Chapter 2

Reflection

Chapter 2

Reflection

Prior to advanced vaccines, childhood diseases were simply a fact of life. When chicken pox struck, a not uncommon rite of passage, how could I have known that it would be a defining moment in Billy's life?

2 Corinthians 4:17
For our light and momentary troubles are achieving for us an eternal glory that far outweighs them all.

My son had just begun fourth grade. As I entered Billy's bedroom to wake him for school, he softly spoke, "Mom, I'm itching everywhere." Sure enough, a flip of the light switch revealed a budding case of chicken pox. I was not alarmed. Actually, I wondered how he had managed to escape it for the past three years as it had spread like wildfire through his elementary school. Billy's tough resistance actually concerned me. I recalled terrible stories of the effects of this particular childhood disease on adults. Now that the inevitable had occurred, I simply hoped for a mild case.

My hope turned to weeks of exhaustion. Within three days, he spiked a high fever which continued for two weeks. An uninterrupted night's sleep was a vague memory. Rumor had it that Epsom Salt baths would relieve the itching. It never really worked. Pockmarks were found in his mouth and in one eye. Ten days into his ordeal, I began to count the blistering raised areas on his face: " Ninety seven, ninety eight, ninety nine." Focused on the task at hand, I totally missed Billy's despair. "Mom, please stop counting. This is not fun." As I held him, I became aware of his rising temperature and then saw tears in his eyes. My heart sank, for Billy rarely cried.

As he buried his face in my arms, I suddenly remembered the smell of his hair when I held him as a baby, a full decade ago. It's funny how a memory can flood back to a precious moment in the nurturing of a child.

The first few months after his birth were a nonstop chorus of crying. The only moments of silence were obtained when I nursed him. Breast feeding or catnaps kept our family dog from howling in unison with Billy's cries. The sound of his screams was unnerving to everyone but me. His wail was simply a reminder that life goes on. I had always dreamed of being a mom.

The day I received the news that I was pregnant with Billy, hopeful anticipation was marred by grief. For six weeks earlier my only sister, Sue had been shot and killed while working at a charity function in New Haven, Connecticut. Her sudden, violent death left our family in a paralyzing limbo of loneliness and heartache. One month prior to her murder, Sue and I spent an afternoon in my kitchen, speculating about our future. She told me that within a year she hoped to have a baby sister for her five year old son Michael. I had miscarried twice. She encouraged me saying, "You'll have a baby, Karen. Just promise me you will enjoy every minute, even the crying!"

My first trimester was a blur of tears and an attempt to make it to work on time. I was a medical assistant at an obstetricians's office. It was terribly difficult not to compare myself with every pregnant woman that was under the care of the doctors. One morning after assisting the doctor with a young woman as she miscarried, I broke down to my co-worker. The words poured out of my mouth, "Why did Sue have to die? Why wasn't it me instead? Sue has a little boy to raise. I have nothing." Missing Sue overpowered every waking hour during that grievous summer of 1983.

The week of Thanksgiving brought me hope that the baby I was carrying would actually make it. As the medical technician emptied the jar of cold gel on my extended belly, he placed the wand in the slimy glop and pointed to the screen. "See, there he is!" We knew I was having a boy. Jim was elated. From that moment forward, my unborn baby consumed my thoughts and hopes. I loved being pregnant. But each time I would feel him kick, my smile would fade into tears, for I longed to share every experience of my long awaited pregnancy with Sue. I now understood fully the emotion described as bitter-sweet.

Staying busy, Jim spent the winter adding a closet to a den for the new nursery. My step-children, Jimmy and Lara, occupied the larger bedrooms in the house. The transformation of our tiny den would be concluded with new coat of paint. Soft beige and whites would be a light and airy backdrop for the life-size colorful wall stickers and red balloon lamp that spruced up the nursery. An overstuffed chair that was in my own bedroom as a child would be placed between the crib and changing table. I now longed to lift my new baby out of his crib and hold him in my arms as I curled up in my chair. I wondered what he look like? Would he have my dark hair and eyes or would he be fair, like his daddy?

Jim had a good part of the winter to complete the nursery. My due date was March 26, 1884. Yet babies do have their own time clocks. On the first of February, I was admitted to the hospital in early labor. Unable to stop the inevitable, our son William Joel Rhea, was born on the afternoon of Groundhog's Day. I pushed unsuccessfully for 3 hours when my obstetrician wisely insisted on a Cesarean Section. A clear internal view revealed that the placenta had grown through my uterus. Apparently William's total form was in full view through my abnormally thin uterus. As the surgeon skillfully delivered our 5 pound, 2 ounce blond baby boy and sutured me back together, she explained that our newborn's umbilical cord was acting like a bungee cord. I was told that I would never be able to carry a baby to full term and that this birth was nothing shy of a miracle.

William and I were released one week later from the hospital. It was hard to imagine how many late nights Jim must have spent completing his nursery. It was my haven. I spent months hobbling around from a nasty inflammation of the sciatic nerve from my back labor. Yet when I entered William's room, I felt rested. Jim would occasionally open the door and yell over baby cries, "I'll be outside putting up fencing." He got a tremendous amount of yard work completed that spring. He entered the house for food and liquids and escaped the high pitched premmie squeals for the solitude of the great outdoors.

Milestones in William's development were to be seared in my mind forever. On Mother's Day I awoke and realized that I had slept through the night for the first time since my son's birth. At three months old he continued to nurse at midnight and 4:00 a.m.. Streaking out of bed, my heart pounded as I envisioned him motionless in the crib. Why had he not awakened? After flinging open the nursery door, I ripped him off the mattress. He laughed out loud. It was his first simulated amusement park ride and he loved it. Feeling like an absolute idiot, I turned toward the telephone with William in my arms and dialed Sue's number to share the moment. On the second ring I slammed down the phone. She was dead. Reduced to tears I could almost hear her voice, "Happy Mother's Day Karen. Your little boy just gave you the gift of sleep." I missed her so much.

When William turned six months old, eight teeth appeared in two days. Following that momentous month, the sleepless nights and endless wailing became a thing of the past. His gentle disposition and sly wit bloomed overnight.

Before two years of age, he would cry if left in the care of anyone other than our family or his grandparents. I didn't do well away from him either, so I stayed by his side for two years! Yet he did spend a tremendous amount of time with my parents, Gwen and Bill Du Bois. His Mimi and Pop, as he called them, were always met with great enthusiasm by their grandson.

Now my dad had a vocabulary that was not for the faint of heart. Obscenities rolled off his tongue in casual, daily conversation. Dad attempted to be careful when in his grandson's presence, but his 63 year old habit was hard to break. I knew better than to try to change him, so I worked with William. I'd explain, "William, _____ is not a nice word. Don't ever say that. Your Pop just can't think of a nicer word to use. Show me how smart you are by thinking of a better, descriptive word." Interestingly enough, William seemed to understand.

At 16 months old, we placed him on the fireplace hearth to capture him on our new video camera. His performance was stellar. "Who is holding the camera, William?" He smiled, "Dada." Jim's voice chimed in, "What's my name?" His sweet baby voice stated, "Jim!" I spoke up. "What's mommy's name?" Williams hands landed on his hips. "Karen." "What's your Pop's name?" He responded, "Bill." Jim asked, "What's your Mimi's name, William?" Looking directly into the lens of the camera with a gleam in his eye and a twisted grin, William announced, "Dammit, Gwen!" This was too good to be true. Captured on video, we gave my parents this priceless evidence for Christmas.

William was definite about his likes and dislikes. His forehead would wrinkle and his lips would pierce in frustration when I continued to call him William. The influence of Jimmy and Lara abounded. By the age of two, he was now officially Billy, and he let everyone know it. His determination and happy temperament remained predictable into elementary school.

Every school day was "The best day ever, mom!" He loved to read and write stories. History, science, math, they were all his passions. His ability to memorize enabled him to achieve excellent test scores. Never quite satisfied with his own age group, he routinely asked older kids about their schools and what they were learning. Billy never lacked an enthusiasm for learning, so he thrived in the classroom. Pushing himself to make it to school when he didn't feel up to par was a given.

Now that Billy was 10 years old there was little doubt that I had one sick kid on my hands. His big blue eyes shed many tears during those trying weeks. It was tough missing the second and third week of fourth grade. He loved school and his teacher. Even though he continued to run a low grade fever, Billy begged to get back to his classroom. I relented, encouraging my little guy to go to the health room if the day felt too long. I wondered what everyone would say? His body was one, big, dried up pockmark. What a sight he was as he stepped up into the school bus after weeks of misery! Turning around, Billy flashed me a big, toothy smile and yelled, "Bye Mom." My "Sweet William" was back.

Chapter 3

Resignation

Chapter 3

Resignation

B illy was no longer a healthy child. He missed school frequently. We needed a doctor to help us find some answers to our questions.

> **John 16:12-13**
> *"I have much more to say to you, more than you can now bear. But when He, the Spirit of truth comes, He will guide you into all truth."*

Billy missed 52 days of school in fourth grade. Fifth grade was more of the same. The doctor's office number was added to my speed dial. It seemed Billy's resistance to infection had been depleted. He caught every cough and cold that came his way. He was placed on antibiotics every six to eight weeks for apparent bronchitis. I must have said it a hundred times, "Billy's immune system seems to have been compromised since he got the chicken pox."

His pediatrician recommended complete testing for

allergies. Following a two-hour visit involving countless pin pricks in his back, the results were definitive. Billy did not have allergies. His constant cough was still unnerving.

Our new HMO medical plan did not include Billy's pediatrician on 'the list' of participating doctors. So we opted for a doctor that was recommended by several close friends. His convenient location was a big consideration. I knew we would be running to his office often in light of Billy's recurrent upper respiratory problems.

The waiting room in Dr. Colton's office was commonly packed with sickly kids and adults. An occasional grumbling patient would scowl, "Great, how late is he running today?" Most patients that walked through the door payed a co-pay prior to their appointment. The receptionist routinely asked if they were covered under the same insurance as the last visit. I was amazed at the numerous insurance plans that Dr. Colton was associated with. It was no wonder that he was so busy. I never complained about the wait, for I hated to think of Dr. Colton dropping his name from our insurance plan to lighten his load. Plus why get upset, for we were always met with a kind, attentive physician who spoke directly to Billy?

Ruling out asthma, Dr. Colton recommended allergy testing with a different allergist he preferred. Not trusting the negative results from the previous year, he pointed out that allergy shots could restore his health. So I acquiesced. Poor Billy. Once again he lay face down on a table and bravely endured the pin pricks in his back and arms.

Surprisingly, the results showed a positive reaction to dust and mold. Jim and I were instructed to rip up his carpet in his bedroom. Information for purchasing a hypo-allergenic mattress, sheets and pillows was provided. Jim installed new hardwood floors. The cost was substantial but worth it. The good news was that the weekly shots could be administered at the office of his primary care physician's office. The cost would be $10.00 a visit instead of the 'specialist' co-pay of $20.00. Thank God for small favors.

Billy was ready and willing for the shots to begin. At least we now had a solid plan of action. Or so we thought.

Chapter 4

Poor Judgment

Chapter 4

Poor Judgment

I learned that momentous occasions with a sick child were an impossible mix of excitement and alternative plans.

Isaiah 55:8
"For my thoughts are not your thoughts, neither are your ways my ways", declares the Lord.

My step-daughter, Lara and her fiancé, Alan, asked Billy to be an usher in their upcoming wedding. The idea of wearing a tuxedo along with his older brother, Jimmy, and four other young men was very exciting. On the night of the rehearsal, Billy put on his suit and tie. Anticipating the instructions concerning his important duties during the ceremony at the church, coupled with dinner at an elegant restaurant, made him feel very grown up. At twelve years old, Billy loved feeling like an adult.

Jim was not concerned when midnight approached, for the late afternoon wedding the next day would give Billy some added time to sleep in the morning. I was more concerned about myself. Eight hours of sound sleep was the only way my mind clearly functioned the next day. The older I got the more reliable my internal time clock became, refusing to let me sleep any later than 7:00 a.m. It seemed that my head barely hit the pillow when Jim and I awoke at the crack of dawn to a female cardinal attacking its own reflection in our bedroom window. Groggy, this particular wake up call was way too early. Lara and Alan's big day had arrived, and even the birds seemed to say, "Get up now!"

I had about six hours remaining before I needed to get myself showered. The morning would allow me the needed time to accomplish a project that awaited my attention. Shortly after lunch Lara had planned to have photographs taken of our family and her attendants on our front porch just prior to the wedding. We were all overjoyed at the clear, sunny September day. The porch had been under construction, and the final chore was to stain our new front door. Actually, I was more thrilled about the cooperative weather for my project than the blue skies for the wedding. So at 7:00 a.m. I began to apply the dark mahogany stain with hopes of its final beauty appearing as a perfect backdrop to the all white wedding apparel in the photograph keepsakes. Jim walked up and handed me my desperately needed mug of coffee. After ingesting ten minutes of caffeine, I returned to the painstaking task of stroking my brush on the edges of the door; avoiding the glass panes. Jim grinned. "Too bad one of the two carriage lamps is on back order." Well into the project, I had forgotten that while one lamp was installed on the upper right corner of the door, the left corner revealed exposed bare wires protruding from the white vinyl siding. I refused to let this imperfection deter my momentum. Laughing, Jim reminded me that we now had two obstacles to consider.

Hopefully the photographer's lens would avoid the

unsightly wires beside the door, and the girls would not brush up against the mahogany stain. Surely it would be tacky for a full 24 hours. Now the bridesmaids would have to maneuver through the mushy grass in their high heels in order to reach the front porch. I knew Lara would take this in stride, as our family had become accustomed to the inconveniences associated with twelve years of constant construction and remodeling. It never interrupted our social life or entertaining, so why should Lara's wedding day be any different? It was part of our existence. Jim had the tenacity needed for physical labor and long hours. Before he finished one project, he would begin to plan another. His eye for design focused on landscaping, fencing, new exterior doors, windows, ceilings, ceramic tile, upgrading bathrooms, additional closet space and an expansion of the kitchen. None of us escaped the ever present sinus conditions associated with drywall dust.

This present job of the front door didn't take nearly as long as I had anticipated. Proudly I stood back and admired the beauty of the newly stained wood. Light headed, the fumes from the stain, or the overload of caffeine from too many mugs of java, were taking their toll. Switching gears, I needed to clean up and grab some cereal and a banana. Getting Billy moving would be a chore. Jim had tried unsuccessfully to wake him. Next it would be my turn to try.

Noon had come and gone as I tried to wake Billy for the third time. After all, he had to eat something, shower and put on his tux. Bending forward, I shook his shoulders, "Billy, you absolutely have to get out of bed!" As he tried to open his eyes, my heart sank. "Mom, I hurt all over." Helping him to his feet and into the bathroom, he stumbled. I knew he was burning up with fever. Glancing at his tuxedo hanging neatly on the doorknob, Jim and I encouraged him. "This is it, Buddy! Your sister and Alan only get married this one day." Drawing a cool bath, I gave him ibuprofen. It was like torture, watching Billy shiver in the tub, but it was a necessary evil to bring down his fever. Crushed ice and juice would hopefully revive him. Pouring him into his tux, he could only be able to watch the ceremony. With sad resignation in his voice, he said, "Oh, no. I don't think I can make the reception." Of all days, how could this be happening?

    I became aware of several voices in my kitchen. Lara and her bridesmaids had arrived. Leaving Billy with Jim, I descended the staircase to help in anyway I could. Each young woman's hair, makeup and nails looked nothing shy of professionally attended to. They piled into the guest bedroom, unveiling their formal satin white gowns. As they peeled off their sweat pants and t-shirts and carefully slid into their dresses, they were instantly transformed into elegant, graceful young ladies. The moment turned frantic. "Oh no, my bra strap is showing!" The gowns were sleeveless and exposed the girl's bare backs, except for a delicate doubled lattice of fabric. Sure enough, we had a problem. Low on the list of my talents, I've never even pretended to be a seamstress. How could I help? Actually the last wedding I attended stretched my ability to improvise. My two piece suit that I planned to wear was never my favorite, for the skirt was knee length. I preferred a longer, sleeker look. Placing a towel around the edge of my underwear to protect my skin, I hot glue gunned the top of the skirt to my panty hose around my hips. Now the skirt flowed at mid-calf. The matching long jacket covered the ridiculous mess. I doubted that the girls in my house would agree to my hot glue gun method of alteration. So instead, I located two dozen tiny safety pins. Once finished, there was not a hint of an undergarment in sight. A unified sigh of relief filled the room. It was now time to pose for the photographer.

    The warmth of the sun and the stillness of the air made the odor of fresh stain stagnate on the porch. The girls in the bridal party lined up for the snapshots and smiled radiantly.

I laughed to myself and hoped no one would keel over from the fumes. But poor Billy. It was time for a few family pictures. Unsteady on his feet, he begged to lie down in the grass. I was so afraid his tux would become soiled, I put a bath towel on the porch and instructed him to sit on it. He managed to pose for two pictures than went into the house. Ten minutes later as we gathered together to leave for the church, I found Billy fast asleep in our sunroom. Jim carried him to the car.

Slumped dejectedly in a chair in the bridal waiting area of Boyds Presbyterian Church, Billy didn't say a word. He was just too sick. Finally it was time to take our seats. Entering the sanctuary with a supreme effort, he held his head high, forced a smile and walked me down the aisle. But once seated, he held my hand as his body uncontrollably shook with fever.

This tiny white clapboard Victorian period sanctuary, founded in 1876, allowed for 100 friends and family to join Lara and Alan on this fine day. I glanced over the altar at my favorite guest: there was a sizable stained glass portrait in deep shades of reds and blues picturing Jesus kneeling in the Garden of Gethsemane. The music began as Lara entered the back of the sanctuary. We all stood, every eye fixed on her stunning beauty. So much for my makeup, as tears smeared my mascara. Here was Lara. The same little girl who was forced to paint the fence one summer, but didn't miss the opportunity to paint one entire leg and foot in whitewash. No, she was no longer twelve. Alan had fallen in love with my step-daughter when they met on a ferry in the Aegean Sea off the coast of Greece while she was studying one summer overseas. It was so terribly romantic. Alan pursued her long distance from his home in Boston, Massachusetts, with phone calls and red roses. His romantic side unfolded further at the wedding. Just before they took their vows, Alan stepped away from the altar and sat down at the piano. An incredibly talented musician, Alan placed his fingers on the keys as the rich melody of the classical composition Claire de Lune rang through this tiny church. Everyone, including Lara, lost composure. This was a day to remember. Rev. Merritt W. Ednie announced. "Alan and Lara, you are now husband and wife. What God has joined together, let no one pull apart, for the two have become one." The guest all stood, but Billy had fallen fast asleep as he curled up on the hard, wooden pew.

It was true. There was no way he could go to the reception. Our home was a two minute drive from the church. Rushing Billy into the house, he wanted to rest in the family room. I slid a pillow under his head and tossed a light weight blanket over his shivering body. Jim provided him a line up of movies in the VCR and a big glass of ice water and saltine crackers at the ready. Glancing back at Billy, guilt stabbed me. This set up was a pitiful substitute for the true care he required. I just didn't know who to call. Everyone we knew had joined us that day. Shaking off my futile attempt for help, I raced out the door in order to not miss the bride and groom's arrival at the reception hall.

Guests asked Billy's where abouts. I must have told twenty-five people about his current illness. With every concerned look, I became defensive about my choice to come to Lara and Alan's reception. I went into my usual dialogue about the countless days over the past two years that Billy remained in bed. After all, he was twelve years old. At least he wasn't vomiting. Stepping away from friends, I went in search of a pay phone. Intermittently, Jim and I called him every hour to hear his voice, reassuring him and ourselves. Then we would return to socializing and sampling tasty hors d'oeuvres around the circular buffet tables. During a well deserved band break, I dashed for the pay phone once again. His weak voice pleaded, "When are you and Dad coming home Mom?" I knew he hoped for an exact hour, but the best I could promise was, "Not long buddy. As soon as the wedding cake is served, we'll be out of here within an hour." Hanging up the receiver I heard my favorite rhythm and blues tune echo through the hall. It took about one minute to shed my momentary concern and find myself on the dance floor once again. My emotions spun out of control. Was Billy upset? Was he asleep? Was his temperature low grade or dangerously rising? Not a moment went by that I didn't hate the fact that he was missing such a fantastic party. Billy did love to dance.

After many farewells, the evening was over. Jim and I raced home as if arriving five minutes earlier would make any difference. Billy was not asleep as I had hoped. Only when we sat with him did he relax and drift off into a feverish slumber.

On Monday, his doctor detected swollen glands all over his body. The diagnosis was mononucleosis; although this was never confirmed with a blood test. On the contrary, two mono blood tests returned normal. Within weeks his spleen was enlarged. Bed rest was recommended. These were easy instructions to follow, for Billy could not will himself to get out of bed.

He missed the first two months of seventh grade. Missing out on his Boy Scout events and youth group activities added to Billy's despair. He couldn't imagine how he would ever be able to make up his school work. I was confident that all would be well, for God had granted my son a bright and focused mind. Truly, my added time with him during his illness was a forced blessing. Billy was always good company.

One afternoon we were thumbing through the photographs from the wedding. Grinning, Billy pointed out the exposed wires from the missing light fixture that was revealed in every single picture on the front porch. It was a gentle reminder of the imperfections of that day. The construction project which consumed me that September morning now seemed so trivial, almost comical. Actually I cringed, remembering my decision to leave my son with a high fever, alone in the house for hours while I laughed and danced away the evening at Lara and Alan's reception; a terribly poor choice that I have grievously regretted over the years. My lack of sound judgement brought me a new conviction in caring for my son. I would never leave him helpless again.

Chapter 5

Provision

Chapter 5

Provision

All it took was one teacher's insensitivity to rob our lives of a little happiness. I'm so exhausted. Fatigue often transfers into stupid words which flow from my mouth. My anger has never defused a volatile encounter.

Psalm 141: 1-3
O Lord, I call to you; come quickly to me. Hear my voice when I call to you. May my prayer be set before you like incense; may the lifting up of my hands be like the evening sacrifice. Set a guard over my mouth, O Lord; keep watch over the door of my lips.

Very few of my son's middle school teachers realized that school was not the only activity Billy missed. His church youth group, Boy Scouts and countless family outings were ruined as he spent yet another day in bed. One of his seventh grade teachers called me to ask why Billy wasn't in class again. As I described his various symptoms, she began to lecture me, explaining that other children came to class with runny noses, tired, or a little nauseated. Furiously I snapped, "Look, he can't lift his head off the pillow this morning." I continued, "You have no idea how adversely Billy's poor health is affecting every aspect of his life."

I was getting nowhere. She told me to consider psychological help and gave me the name of an "excellent" child psychologist. She said that it may be hard to digest because we all think our children are perfect, but possibly Billy didn't like school. To hammer her case home, she asked, "Aren't you concerned that your son doesn't have one special friend?" "Well, duh!!" I thought to myself, "He's never there." I lashed out at her and said her college Psychology 101 was not going to wash with me. Stating that she didn't need to be subjected to my verbal abuse, she hung up on me.

Livid, I paced through my kitchen. Suddenly a pang of guilt rushed over me. I had been terribly harsh with his teacher. Why did I allow myself to be so condescending with the Psychology 101 comment? I'm sure she saw me as unapproachable for the remainder of the school year. Yet the lack of dialogue between the two of us may have been a good thing. Her opinion of Billy had been formed before we ever spoke on the phone. Regardless, there would be more important battles ahead.

One of my son's most fulfilling weeks was spent attending Space Camp in Huntsville, Alabama, during elementary school. Each year he longed to return to try out their new Florida location. Now in middle school, he would be placed in the more advanced space class. This educational camp is an excused absence throughout school districts in the United States. Even though Billy had missed dozens of days due to illness, the planning had begun.

His knowledge and love of the planets, the solar system

and the universe started when he was four years old. He memorized every fact regarding the planet's temperatures, number of moons, and their distances to earth. His first science fair in elementary school sent us racing to the craft store for styrofoam balls, wire and paint. His dad helped him produce a mobile of the planets, complete with labels stating various facts.

Our family watched the movie "The Right Stuff" numerous times in our home. The space race simply intrigued our son. His love of reading and of select movies (history and science fiction) kept him occupied during his many, many weeks in bed. Jim and I looked at Space Camp as a further opportunity for Billy to succeed and excel in the sciences. We naturally assumed his science teacher would be just as enthusiastic. We were wrong.

I was learning what the word 'flexibility' actually meant. Jim had been on a mission trip to the Amazon Basin, providing much-needed dental care to the Peruvian people. He was due back the evening before the three of us planned to hop on the auto train and head for Florida. While Billy absorbed five days of space information, Jim and I would tour St. Augustine, Florida. This would afford a short drive back to Space Camp at Cape Kennedy if Billy should become sick. We planned a leisurely drive back to Maryland the following weekend.

The evening Jim was due to arrive home, the phone rang. Over crackling static I heard my husband's faint voice saying, "I will not be home in time to catch the auto train to Florida." He was stuck in Lima's airport with no hope of getting to the U.S. for another two days. I was terribly disappointed, but not nearly as upset as Jim. Billy and I were to deal with the train alone and find our way to Cocoa Beach, Florida. Jim would try to meet up with me at our hotel.

By the time Billy got home from school, I was emotionally worked up. As I greeted him at the back door, I could see he was also upset. As I dragged the luggage out of the basement, my mind was fixed on Jim's predicament. "What's wrong, Buddy?" I asked. Following me around the house as I packed, he described in detail a conversation he had just had with his science teacher regarding his upcoming week at Space Camp. Billy gathered the essential class work from each and every teacher for his travel days. However, his science teacher refused to give him the assigned work saying, "The number of your absences has helped me to arrive at the decision that your week at Space Camp will not be excused and you will surely fail science."

Furious, I picked up the phone and called his guidance counselor. She was of no help and actually told me that Billy's teacher may have a point. I reminded her that this camp was an approved absence and had been arranged five months earlier. Getting nowhere, I informed her that a letter would be in the mail to the principal. As I hung up the phone, Billy walked into the room with slumped shoulders, expressing his opinion that we should possibly cancel his week away from school. He burst out in tears and said, "Mom, I just can't fail science!" I assured him that his teacher was an idiot, and I would not permit him to receive a failing grade. It may not have been the most genteel response, but it was the only answer I could muster up.

To add to this day's craziness, Billy felt we should get his dad's opinion. Now I had to tell him that his dad was stuck in Peru and would not be able to meet us in Florida until several days later. Looking at one another, we actually started to laugh. Pulling ourselves together, we madly packed the Jeep and examined the Florida map. By the time we boarded our sleeper car on the train, I took a long look at Billy's once bright, blue eyes and saw nothing but grey. He was getting sick. Aching from head to toe, his throat hurt when he swallowed. At least he could sleep on the bunk bed until the following morning.

Well, God is good. Against all odds, Jim actually beat us to the hotel. Billy and I felt awfully good about our travel adventure. We packed well and never got lost. Space Camp was difficult, for fatigue and body aches caused Billy to miss numerous activities, but he did manage to stay the five planned days. And yes, he passed science.

Chapter 6

Absentee Compassion

Chapter 6

Absentee Compassion

I counted down the remaining days of the school year with the anticipation of a child. The warmth of the sun, cookouts, the fragrance of fresh cut grass, family vacations and Billy's camp were around the corner. Finally the stress of continual makeup work from multiple absences in school would end. The slower pace of summer was near.

Galatians 6:2
Carry each other's burdens, and in this way you will fulfill the law of Christ.

Billy talked of little else but attending a five-day outdoor Christian concert in Pennsylvania. The end of June couldn't arrive any faster. He and his close friends would be camping out with several adults who always volunteered their time and talents for our church's numerous enthusiastic preteens. Adding to his excitement, his favorite musical group would be performing, along with other quality speakers and musicians.

Yet springtime gave way to an increased string of absences and antibiotic treatments for chronic tonsilitis. The surgeon scheduled Billy's tonsillectomy just two weeks prior to trip. He believed that recovery would take one week, and then Billy would feel 100 percent better than before. After our consultation, Jim and I became swept up in our son's excitement. Jim questioned why we weren't going along as well. An experienced back-packer and camper, he loved an adventure. But I quickly reminded him that the idea of hiking to public restrooms and loading on bug spray to no avail sounded like pure misery to me. We agreed that the adults in our son's charge were surely more prepared for the week than I would ever be.

Unfortunately, just days away from the trip, Billy's recuperation was not going as hoped. In terrible pain, he sipped constantly on liquids, wincing in pain with each swallow. As he loaded salt on his chicken broth, I believed that the added sodium would help him to heal. He could barely whisper. Seven days after his surgery the doctor prescribed more codeine after seeing his raw throat. Well into the refill of pain killers, Jim and I wondered how we could possibly let him go away.

Then two days prior to leaving, Billy pulled himself together, forcing meals down and adopting an upbeat demeanor. We hated to see him miss another activity. His constant disappointments were so hard to witness. Just days away I wondered how he would survive the heat and busy pace. Jim decided to help him pack and make a final decision after getting a true sense of his energy level.

The bedroom floor was piled with T-shirts, shorts, rain gear, bathing suit, a flashlight and personal items, including five pairs of underwear and socks. I caught Jim and Billy snickering as they counted the underwear I laid out for packing. Jim reminded me of the previous summer when Billy returned from Boy Scout Camp. There were way too many pairs of nicely folded jockeys. "Mom, all guys know to turn underwear inside out, and that's how you get another few days out of one pair!" I wanted to believe that an added year would make a difference in my son's away-from-home hygiene. Actually I always breathed a sigh of relief following laundry day after camp-outs!

Billy's energy and wit had returned. Deciding to let our son go brought us great relief. We saw him off, along with a caravan of vans in our church parking lot. Each vehicle practically pulsated with excitement as they began their three hour drive to listen to inspirational speakers, hear live music and camp with all their friends.

The night before the youth group returned, Billy called us at 10:00 p.m. I could hear a profound urgency in his voice. "Please come and get me. I've been throwing up and they wouldn't let me call you." Trying to reassure him was pointless. I listened helplessly as he began dry heaving. Finally one of the chaperones took the cell phone from his hand. She felt he had a virus. I asked her to immediately take him to the infirmary, suspecting dehydration. I reminded her of his complications following his tonsillectomy. Our conversation ended. Hours went by, yet we heard nothing of our son's condition. How could I have not asked for her cell number? I tore apart Billy's room, as well as my own pile of papers, looking for the letter that contained an emergency number. I came up empty handed. The wait was agonizing.

Finally at midnight, a friend came to our rescue with a cell number of an attending adult. This conversation confirmed that our wishes had not been acted upon. My husband lost his temper when Billy was unable to talk on the phone because the dry heaving was so severe. Demanding that our request be honored, Jim asked if anyone had offered Billy a drink containing electrolytes earlier that evening. Juice was repeatedly offered to him, but they were missing the point of the necessity of electrolytes to re-hydrate our son.

Before hanging up the phone, the leader said our son was acting defiantly, adding that she made it a rule to never respond to the demands of a child. She further added that he had been very rude. In outrage, we pressed, "In the two years you've known Billy, has he ever been disrespectful?" After a long pause, she said she would get him to the medical tent.

While Jim and I paced and stared at the phone, we couldn't believe what was happening. Surely someone in the group was aware that behavior changes, vomiting and diarrhea were all indications of dehydration. Billy knew he was very ill. We prayed for divine intervention.

An hour dragged by and we heard nothing. Restless, Jim grabbed the map. We searched and plotted a route to get to Billy. Yet once we arrived, how would we locate his youth group amongst the tens of thousands in attendance? Furious at the whole situation, we paced and stared at the phone. If only it would ring with a skilled medical person on the other line.

Two hours later the telephone rang. Sure enough, once examined by an EMT, Billy was placed on an IV. The vomiting and dry heaving was so severe that an antiemetic suppository had to be administered. How humiliating this must have been for my thirteen-year-old son. The EMT said that Billy was brought in terribly dehydrated. His blood pressure was dangerously low but now was slowly rising. He was sleeping peacefully. We were discouraged from driving through the night to pick him up. The EMT was very reassuring, believing Billy could rest well and be able to ride home with his church group in the morning.

Nine hours later, as Billy struggled out of the church van, we were berated by one of the chaperones, "You have no idea how far we had to walk to get to the infirmary." She continued, "There was a teen in the infirmary with a broken limb." Driving home her point to minimize Billy's situation, she added, "I do hope you will send a generous donation to the medical personnel that volunteered at the event. It's not cheap to hook a kid up to an IV."

Later that evening as I tossed all of my son's clothes from his trip into the washing machine, counting clean underwear was a minimal concern. I contemplated how doubly upsetting the past 24 hours had been. It was so hurtful first to be ignored and then let down, especially within the Body of Christ. I recalled an old pastor of mine chuckling as he said, "I'd love my job, if it wasn't for all the people!" Yes, even believers fall short in the mercy and grace department. Keeping my eyes fixed on God, and not on the circumstances of the previous night, was hard.

Chapter 7

A Dad's Dedication

Chapter 7

A Dad's Dedication

How tempting it is to drop out of living life when a child is sick. Be encouraged to take heart and stay focused. Your work and determination will bless your family, as well as those you have been called to serve.

> **Philippians 2:4-5**
> *Each of you should look not only to your own interest, but also to the interests of others. Your attitude should be the same as that of Christ Jesus.*

Boy Scouts was Billy's passion and therefore it became my husband's delight. After many weekends spent in extensive training, Jim became the High Adventure Assistant Scout Master for Troop 496. The Adirondacks in New York State was the older boys' destination. Countless weekends were spent preparing for the backpacking and canoeing adventure that lay ahead.

Unfortunately, Billy missed more 'shake downs' and

preparatory 'treks' than he attended. Underweight, fatigued and often dehydrated, the physical demands were more than our son could endure. How many times did I stand in our driveway and witness Jim forcing himself to be upbeat for the other nine boys in training? Before hopping into his Jeep, Jim would turn to me and whisper, "This stinks. I can't believe Billy is missing another weekend." The two men in my life had so many disappointments.

While Jim was gone, Billy and I would fall into a routine of relaxing. "Do you want to watch a movie, Buddy?" He'd respond with, "How about some popcorn with lots of salt?" Two hours later he'd be a bit more energetic. We'd talk about what the guys were up to at that particular moment in time. Tired of talking, Billy would retire to his bedroom for hours. He loved to read and write, so at least his escape was a healthy one. If he couldn't hike and camp, he'd continue to learn. I was more concerned about my husband than Billy.

At the appointed hour when Jim and the scouts returned, a half dozen parents would arrive to pick up their sons. Now I could read my husband, and there was no faking it. He had a great time. These wonderful parents never missed an opportunity to tell me what an incredible man my husband was. Their praises of his positive influence over their boys filled me with pride. They were very aware of how hard it must have been for Jim to go on so many outings without his own son. One mom pointed out, "My husband would have given up this responsibility months ago." They thanked us over and over again for his dedication.

After Jim unloaded his gear and the last parent left, he would express his frustration and disappointment that Billy was missing out once again. Then with a twinkle in his eye, he would spend the next hour telling us hysterically funny stories about this band of young men. Each boy had different strengths and weaknesses. One never tied his shoes. Another purposely walked and splashed in every puddle and stream. Someone always forgot toilet paper or a flashlight. One kid was a natural comedian, commanding the stage at the nightly campfire. And all were winning my husband's heart.

Well, Billy finally did make it to the Adirondacks. Equipped and closely watched over by his dad and fellow scouts, Billy climbed the highest peak in New York State, Mt. Marcy. He still had his off days, but, all in all, this major accomplishment and many to come were due to his father's belief that he had a responsibility for all the boys in his charge. My husband was being observed by the scouts, their parents and Billy. I believe the Lord was surely pleased with His servant, Jim Rhea.

Chapter 8

Music Silenced

Chapter 8

Music Silenced

Why are kids so cruel? I've seen children in the throws of adolescence behave like a pack of wolves. They target a weak classmate as they move in for the kill. I often wondered, "Who is in charge?"

> **Colossians 4:5**
> *Be wise in the way you act toward outsiders; make the most of every opportunity. Let your conversation be always full of grace, seasoned with salt, so that you may know how to answer everyone.*

Billy approached his advancement to middle school with great anticipation. He had played the violin since age five and looked forward to the opportunities an organized orchestra would provide. His continuing illness had unforeseen consequences for his violin playing. For some reason, while attempting to play the violin, the tips of his fingers would bleed, causing terrible pain. Antibiotic cream and bandaids on every finger became the norm. Yet Billy's resolve was unshaken. He couldn't wait to perform at his school and be a part of our county's honors orchestra.

Advancement to seventh grade included long orchestra practices and a new private violin instructor that agreed to see only serious students. He was an elderly, no nonsense gentlemen with kind eyes. Billy greatly admired his teacher's skill and wanted to please him by excelling in technique and various assigned sheets of music. Instead, over the next six months, my son would seem distracted and unable to practice. After being reprimanded by his teacher for failing to play a piece properly, Billy hopped in the car announcing that he hated the violin. He slept the rest of the way home. I chalked up his frustration to the intensity of the new demands being placed on him.

Jim and I were not going to let him quit. He seemed to be going through the identical frustration and boredom that my aunt had warned me about a decade earlier. I was in awe of my younger cousins' musical talents. When I questioned their mom about the kids' abilities, she explained that every summer the children were allowed to choose which instrument they wanted to play for the entire year. Some years were smooth sailing, while others held the possibility of a non-stop rooster fight had it not been for the rule of non-negotiation in their home. If one hated the piano, harp or sax after a few months, she told them to be thinking about which instrument would be fun, and they would discuss it at the beginning of the summer. Year after year the kids learned to stop complaining, for she wouldn't budge. One child would stick with the same instrument for four years or more. The other changed annually. Consequently, these children were well disciplined, talented and excelled in school. Jim and I believed we were witnessing Billy in the throws of typical adolescent defiance. Yes, he would play the violin, and we would discuss a possible change of instrument the following summer.

Weekly, as we drove 30 minutes to his private lesson, my son was unusually quiet. I believed he was nervous, as he rarely took the time required for practice. Then I became aware that he started forgetting to take his violin to school. His dad and I reminded him that his years of practice and performing showed maturity and sacrifice. Also, the financial investment for his violin wasn't cheap. We had invested thousands of dollars into violins, lessons and music. In fact his present violin was purchased the previous summer. Plus I was tired of getting calls from Billy while I was at work. I reminded Billy that a forgotten violin never constituted an emergency. Apologizing, he would plead with me to leave the office and bring in his violin so he could practice with the orchestra. A friend suggested that he had Attention Deficit Disorder. Maybe she was right. He was forgetful and his room was a wreck. I began to read up on ADD.

When I was at work and there were no patients in the waiting room, I would update my journal. It was filled with Billy's latest physical problems, currents medications and an entry or two of his problems at school. I wrote, "I haven't received a call from Billy at school in six weeks. He just seems so unhappy. Maybe we are being too rigid about sticking with the violin until the summer."

Some of Jim's young patients at his dental practice included several fellow students from our son's middle school. A typical afternoon found our waiting room filled with school age children. The bus would drop off Billy at the end of our driveway. He always made a point to pop his head in the waiting room, come around the desk and give me a quick run down of the events of his day before going to the kitchen for a snack. Today was different. Billy opened the door and simply waved after seeing our next patient and her mom getting out of their car. He hurried by me and climbed the stairs into the house.

His classmate walked in and began to cry. When her mom asked what was wrong, her daughter turned to me and wailed, "Is Billy Okay?" As her account of the day unfolded, she told me the frightening details of witnessing Billy being beat up in the hall by three boys. My husband and I discovered that while Billy fought the increasing pain from the rawness in his fingers, he was being punched and kicked on a daily basis. Their final insult was to toss his violin down the hall, concluding their assault with crude insults. I ran upstairs to find him asleep in the sunroom. Bruises were evident on his face. It was no wonder Billy was leaving his violin at home. Believing our intervention would only make things worse, Billy pleaded with us to not get involved. Yet we knew adult intercession was a must.

Sitting in the principal's office, Jim and I sat dumbfounded as he suggested peer mediation for all the boys to try to resolve their differences. We could not fathom the merit in subjecting Billy to meeting with these bullies. Jim and I were in such agreement that we finished each other's sentences. Also, it was ridiculous to pull our son out of his classes for their mediation sessions. Instead, my husband requested a meeting with the boys' parents. That request was met with a blatant, "No, that would not be appropriate." Upon our exit, the principal said, "Listen, why don't you buy him a second violin, keeping one at school and one at home for practice." He smiled as he added, "Maybe he won't look like such a target."

Had this moment magically transformed into animation, the principal would have witnessed steam exploding out of our ears, as Jim and I produced enormous mallets in hand. Taking turns, we would pound him, a foot at a time into the earth below. Actually, we exited his office and dashed to the parking lot. We exploded in verbal rage in the privacy of our car. How could we deal with a principal that was no doubt a bully with a degree? I thought back to Billy's silence over the months, as he listened to his dad and me lecture him about his commitment to the violin. I was furious for my kid.

Praying for my son's tormentors felt like a prayer of David from Psalms. "Smite them, O God." My imagination raged. I envisioned entering the lunch room and having Billy point out the school thugs. As one smugly leaned back on his chair, I would come up from behind. As my hands tightened around his throat, he would scream for mercy and begin to cry as I would announce in a deep, threatening voice, "Don't you ever touch my kid again." I pictured releasing my grip and swiftly flipping my foot toward the remaining chair leg touching the floor. Walking away, a crash would sound as the obnoxious kid hit the deck. A roar of laughter would fill the lunch room. This was only illusional satisfaction! Suddenly my ugly thoughts would turn against those in authority.

I finally acknowledged that my vivid, dark imagination was no less pleasing to the Lord, than our son's unprincipled principal who enabled the ugly actions and words of Billy's adolescent classmates. Jim and I needed to devise a plan of protection for our son. So we decided to pull Billy out of school midyear and enrolled him in a less stressful Montessori School. Jim and I were stuck in a conversational replay for months, wondering why good kids have to leave public education in order to be safe? I still feel outrage, thinking of the countless children who live in fear every day.

My intentions were to contact the Board of Education, filing a formal complaint regarding Billy's principal. I never did. I had a sick kid, and there was simply no time. His transfer to a safe school was a wise decision. Unfortunately a music program was not in their curriculum. He hadn't picked up his violin in months, but his fingers continued to bleed and his hands would peel. Caring for his physical deterioration filled my days and nights. At least his new teachers were compassionate. His new schedule and friends were met with ease. He and his new buddy, Lyndsay shared the same wit, intellect and ability to pretend, as if they were still little boys. The school battle was finally over.

Billy's instrument went into its case and was stored in the basement with his quarter size and half size violins. He never played again.

Chapter 9

Hindering Help

Chapter 9

Hindering Help

∽

I began educating myself medically, challenging my son's doctor. When he failed to seriously consider Billy's mounting symptoms, I began surfing the net for possible illnesses. Suggesting certain possibilities, he soon became sick of my homespun research. After all, he was the physician.

> **2 Thessalonians 3:13**
> *And as for you, brothers, never tire of doing what is right.*

By the age of thirteen, Billy's health was terribly compromised. I had insisted on receiving a referral to a surgeon who could remove his tonsils and adenoids. The antibiotic treatments to which he was constantly subjected were not working. After this operation, his surgeon commented that he had never seen such a terrible hidden infection in 30 years of practice. No wonder his resistance had been so run down. Maybe now he would feel better.

Within months, however, our hopes for improved health were shattered when his cough and sore throats returned.

New problems surfaced. Terribly weak, Billy could no longer climb the steps to his bedroom. He would sit on the bottom step and scoot backwards until he reached the top of the staircase. Chronic urinary tract infections became the norm. His body ached terribly. The diagnosis was allergies and growing pains. Once, Dr. Colton met me in the parking lot and told me not to bother bringing Billy inside. He handed me a sample medication of a popular antihistamine. He said the weather system created by El Nino was affecting everyone; and if we agreed to resume allergy shots, Billy would feel better. Jim and I felt his suggestion was misguided.

I wondered if he had Lyme's Disease. His symptoms fit. Between hikes with his scout troop and living on a farm, Billy had been in contact with his share of ticks. Even though the blood tests were normal, I had read many stories of false results. I even called the Center for Disease Control in Georgia and discussed my suspicions with one of their experts on several diseases caused by different types of ticks. So we had Billy on the recommended low dose of antibiotics for months. His skin took on a greyish, bronze tone. This was attributed to an antibiotic burn; a reaction in the skin to the treatment. We were grasping at straws as we desperately searched for answers.

I asked if Billy might have juvenile rheumatoid arthritis. It was the first time Dr. Colton became visibly angry with me. He told me to leave the examination room and said Billy could no longer be seen if I was present. Tossing a referral in front of me, he told me I was costing him money with all the numerous monthly referrals and, furthermore, wasting everyone's time. He stormed into the next examination room to get away from me and see his next patient.

Weeks later, Billy and I met with the specialist. I found him to be quite arrogant. I thought, "I don't need to socialize with his man. I just want him to find out why Billy is so fatigued with achy joints." After briefly examining Billy, he said, "Nothing is wrong with your son." Angry, I suspected that a previous "heads up" had been prearranged between these two doctors. I pushed, "Isn't there a blood test that would confirm or deny my suspicions?" He said he didn't do blood work-ups; I would need to get a referral for a lab test from my primary care physician. When Billy ducked in the bathroom, the doctor said, "Give it up. You're making your son believe he's sick."

Beginning to doubt my own sanity, I took Billy to a psychiatrist. Yes, Billy was depressed, mainly because he didn't feel well. Observing that Billy was a pretty well adjusted ninth grader, the doctor prescribed an antidepressant. Explaining that depression can manifest itself as debilitating physical symptoms was enough to convince me to begin the medication. I never saw an improvement.

During the winter of Billy's freshman year in high school, the arrogance of Dr. Colton produced a blatant error. Once again, I took my son in for treatment. Abnormally weak, Billy's face seemed puffy and one eye was red. A head cold was the diagnosis. "Keep him home from school and buy an over-the-counter antihistamine." I followed the doctor's advice. Late that same afternoon, Billy was laid out on the love seat. His face, lips and eyes were very swollen. His speech was slurred. I immediately called his doctor. After asking what medication I had given him, I was reprimanded for not checking the label. "The antidepressant that you are giving him," he said, "is an incompatible MAOI inhibitor. He is having a drug reaction." Upset, I asked what I should do? Dr. Colton assured me that Billy would feel better the next morning and he would surely rest well with all the medications I had given him. Hanging up the phone, I stood in the middle of my kitchen, stunned. I truly did not understand what I had done to make Billy worse. Opening the medicine cabinet, the label of his cold tablets stated Dr. Colton's words MAOI inhibitor under its drug interaction precaution. Horrified, I told Jim what I had done. He was furious. "You've got to stop running to the doctor and giving Billy all this crap!" No doubt, I had blown it.

The following morning at 7:00 a.m., I couldn't get Billy out of bed. His lips were abnormally full and his eyes were swollen shut. He wasn't speaking clearly. Calling for Jim, I knew something was terribly wrong. Jim's blood pressure cuff revealed an alarmingly low 80/42. Carrying Billy to the bathroom, Jim yelled for me to call his doctor.

Noticeably agitated, Dr. Colton told me to come by his office and pick up some samples of an antibiotic. Over the telephone, his doctor said, "Billy has a sinus infection." Outraged, Jim & I knew we had to get him to another doctor, but we first had to get permission from our insurance company. Calling, I was transferred to a nurse who asked Billy's history. After putting me on hold, she returned and said, "Get your son to the emergency room, immediately." She explained that two medications I had given Billy the previous day would not cause swelling and slurred speech. She added that Dr. Colton was incorrect in his assessment of one of the medications being a MAOI inhibitor drug. His antidepressant and the cold medication were never the problem. Before we hung up she warned me that the attending physician in the emergency room would, more than likely, consult with Dr. Colton, Billy's primary care physician.

She was correct in her assumption. The attending emergency room physician looked in his eyes, nose and mouth. Within one minute, he concurred that it was a sinus infection, requiring antibiotics. Jim voiced how ridiculous his assessment was. Jim added, "One of his eyes is totally dilated and his blood pressure is dangerously low." The ER doctor said that he probably was not eating or drinking because he was sick and should be on an antibiotic. I asked if the doctor if he could see how swollen Billy's eye lids, face and lips were. Shrugging his shoulders, the doctor once again stated, "He has a sinus infection." We were dismissed.

Jointly, Jim and I decided to hold off on the antibiotic prescribed until Billy was seen by another medical practice. It was time to find a new doctor.

Chapter 10

What Childhood?

Chapter 10

What Childhood?

There are doctors who are truly brilliant and kind. I will no longer settle for less. For if I am not my child's advocate, who will be?

> **Proverbs 3:27**
> *Do not withhold good from those who deserve it, when it is in your power to act.*

It was the first time I met her. After spending ten minutes with my fifteen year old son, this gentle, soft spoken pediatrician asked me to step into the hallway, outside the examination room. Now a tremor in her voice revealed her deep-seated outrage. "This is *not* a sinus infection. Immediately discontinue the antibiotic the ER doctor prescribed yesterday." I let her know that it was never started. As she promised to arrange appointments with the best specialists in the area, I broke down crying. This was the first time in five years that a doctor clearly saw what I had seen all along.

As she began to question me on his medical history, I whipped out my personal catalog of Billy's unhappy saga dated and detailed from years ago. It described the onset of severe fatigue, joint aches, swollen glands, a chronic cough, puffy eyes and lips, headaches, low weight and dehydration. I explained that his eyes would dilate differentially, one then the other, impairing his vision. Very low blood pressure kept him light headed and weak. His speech would slur. His skin tone was grey, almost bronze. Mentally confused and forgetful, his grades plummeted in ninth grade. Depression set in. Before proceeding with any referral appointments, her colleague, Dr. Witmer, explored the possibility of infectious diseases, taking more definitive blood, stool and urine samples. All had normal results, except for an elevated CPK. This indicated stress on the muscles and heart. Our next step was a consultation with a top-notch neurologist in Washington, D.C.

This was not the way I envisioned my son's freshman year of high school. Prep school was academically stimulating for Billy. He made the honor roll his first quarter, yet the rewards were few and far between. All students were strongly encouraged at the beginning of the school year to become involved in extra-curricular activities. So Bill joined the golf team.

We bought him a used set of left-handed clubs and headed for the driving range. He was a natural with a club in his hand, just like my dad. But all of his ability never reached full potential. Following a few sweltering afternoons on the golf course with his school's team, Billy was left ill and dehydrated. His absences began. His golf coach, who was also his science teacher, took an interest in him. On several occasions he speculated with me about the possibility of Billy having a rare disease of some sort. His coach shared, "It's not as though he doesn't have the desire or the ability to participate. Your son is very bright and determined. The doctors must be missing something."

The second quarter proved to be a daily struggle. Billy longed to stay active, but dropped off the golf team. He always laughed at himself and said that the only sports he was any good at did not involve handling a ball. He was an excellent swimmer and snow skier. So in January of his freshman year, he joined the ski club at his school on a weekend bus trip to Vermont. After arriving home, he complained that the new ski boots we bought him were too tight and he couldn't ski well. His feet actually looked swollen to me. Billy made it to school about twice a week for the next two months. He could no longer keep up academically. It was now time to withdraw Billy from high school.

The spring of 1999 would prove to be a season of heart-wrenching speculations and testing. The neurologist mentioned the possibility of Mitochondrial Disease. He explained that this condition caused a cellular breakdown in the body. That evening I walked into Billy's room and noticed that he was glued to his computer screen. Trying to see what had captured his attention, the screen revealed the very disease the doctor mentioned. The word *fatal* appeared. We both sat and wept.

Instead of history, math and English, Billy became an expert on MRI's, EEG's, EMG's, IVP's and the agony of an invasive muscle biopsy to explore his genetic makeup. This biopsy involved a surgical procedure that sliced deep into the muscle of his upper thigh. The test results would take two months to complete. His downhill slide seemed to accelerate after the surgery.

On the Sunday afternoon of his annual Boy Scout troop's banquet, Billy became severely dehydrated and ended up in the ER. The nurse smiled and told us that Billy would be re-hydrated and ready to go home within three hours. Her prediction was not to be. He was never discharged from the emergency room. Instead, after being admitted in the middle of the night, his kidneys began to shut down. Knowing that we were awaiting results from extensive testing, the attending doctor's only added insight was, "This seems to be autoimmune in nature." Billy did not come home until *three* days later.

The following Sunday as our family sat in church, exhaustion swept over me. I had not slept well in months. Usually worship energized me. Not this time. I could have fallen asleep at any moment. A soloist began to sing as the offering plate was passed around the sanctuary. I dug through my purse for my check. Luckily I had filled it out the night before. The usher handed me the plate, as I was sitting on the aisle. I tossed my check in. Before I knew what happened, the usher burst out laughing. Jim leaned over me smiling and whispered to the usher, "Shhhhhhh! She's sleeping, you'll wake her." I had thrown my check into the plate of bread. It was communion. We giggled like unruly school kids for the rest of the service.

I suppose we laughed so seldom anymore, that my fatigue and the absurdity of putting money on top of the blessed unleavened bread made us appear giddy and in love to those around us. On the contrary, I knew our family was becoming unglued.

July was upon us as I steeled myself for the diagnosis from the muscle biopsy. At least we would no longer be faced with the unknown.

Chapter 11

A Marriage In Crisis

Chapter 11

A Marriage In Crisis

I'm no longer my husband's lover and friend, only the caretaker of my sick child. It wasn't always this bad. How will our marriage ever survive?

Matthew 12:25
Jesus knew their thoughts and said to them, "Every kingdom divided against itself will be ruined, and every city or household divided against itself will not stand."

The stress of our son's constant health problems was fracturing our marriage to the very core. Dr. Colton managed to pit my husband against me the previous year, concluding that my son seemed emotionally and physically weak only when he was in my presence. Often that perception was confirmed, for Billy seemed less symptomatic when he was with his dad. The silence in our home was intolerable.

When my husband became angry he simply left the room. Jim would do anything to avoid confrontation.

Growing up in an unhappy home, he told me of the long hikes and horseback rides he would take in order to get away from his parents' fighting. At night, in the solitude of his bedroom, he would lock the door and escape in the pages of a good book. His coping skills as a child were some of the qualities that attracted me to Jim when we met.

But initially it was his easy laugh and irreverent humor that swept me off my feet. Before we were married, Jim had trained me as his dental assistant. Our friendship and subsequent love story began after working an 11 hour day in the office. I went to seat our last patient. A glass window separated the front desk from the waiting room. The child of our next patient had his face plastered up against the window and was smearing his tongue on the glass for an added gross effect. Fatigue got the best of me, and I burst out laughing. Returning to Jim's private office, I told him I couldn't seat the last patient of the day until he came out and saw this kid at the window. Now Jim lost it too, and we huddled in his private office with tears coming down our face. Getting his composure first, Jim told me to take a deep breath and seat this woman so we could go home. After several failed attempts, I finally brought back this very serious woman and placed the bib around her neck. She had a filling to be done on a front tooth. After numbing the area, Jim prepared the tooth for the composite filling. Looking at me, with total professionalism, he said, "Dry the area." Picking up the high pressured air syringe, I tapped the button. Missing the tooth entirely, I blew a jet of air straight up this poor woman's nose. Her eyes popped open, as the forced air totally cleared out her sinus cavity. Professionalism flew out the window, as Jim and I died laughing. How he ever finished the filling, I'll never know. I'm sure the poor lady found a new dentist. But at her expense, I found the love of my life.

After we were married, our lives revolved around the his kids. We did take time for ourselves, which made for sweet memories. Those first two years of marriage were a confirmation of our differences. Jim preferred small intimate gatherings, good literature, horseback riding, traveling, Shakespeare, gardening, hiking, swimming and white water rafting. Growing up on a farm, his family kept all the animals outside. Meticulous with his surroundings and organized, Jim held to the adage: Everything has its place and everything should be in its place. Yet fashion and clothing were low on his list of priorities. He disliked 'chatting' on the telephone. Often ignoring the phone's persistent ringing, he stated, "I'm sure it's for you." Yes, we were opposites.

I loved to telephone friends and family. Jim never understood what I could possibly talk about for so long and suggested that I have the receiver surgically implanted in my ear. Notes, mail, magazines, photos, scissors, car keys and important papers were strategically placed in various piles around the house. *Usually* I could put my hands on the item I was searching for. I enjoyed entertaining, sizeable parties, movies and over sized popcorn, musical theater, reading 'page turners' and snow skiing. Browsing in furniture stores energized me. My winter clothes and summer clothes were frequently mixed together in the closet, as were sizes 10-14 for my various weights. Growing up, our dogs had the run of the house. So did our pet squirrel monkey that lived in my sister's bedroom. Our personalities and our ideas of *normal* were as different as the seasons of summer and winter.

Slowly our individual interests began to rub off on one another. Jim taught me to horseback ride, western style. We loved to go for long horseback rides in the woods. As we ate our picnic lunch, he would share his love of history or catch me up on the latest book he was reading. After mounting our horses we would race competitively across a field toward home. We loved snow skiing and now and then played nine holes of mediocre golf. He took me to musicals and I became exposed to Shakespeare, on stage. I saw every Civil War battlefield from Louisiana to Pennsylvania. Jim learned to find his way out of a mall without hyperventilating. Our dogs and cats took up residence inside the house, much to his chagrin. Sometimes we would have small groups of friends to the house for dessert. But often we'd have big back yard barbeques or throw an occasional pig roast. Jim attended my family reunions in Arkansas and genuinely loved my family. Routinely, my parents and in-laws, Gaye and Guy, would spend Sunday afternoons visiting. Being together added to our enjoyment of continued family traditions. Our individualities remained distinct, as new similarities surfaced. We became comfortably predictable in each other's eyes.

After house hunting for a year, we purchased our fixer-upper home with a bit of acreage. Visions of seasonal upkeep and the remodeling that awaited us was a great attraction. A lover of accomplished goals, Jim could single handedly design and build an addition to our new house. He turned our plain front yard into a visual feast of dogwood trees, bushes, seasonal flowers and two fish ponds, complete with waterfalls. I enjoyed mowing, interior painting and basically being his spare pair of hands. All in all, Jim had endless energy and an adventurous spirit. I was able to keep up with him because I was a tad industrious and truly enjoyed his company. We were quite a team.

When Billy was in second grade, our weekly outings on our horses came to abrupt halt. Billy and I had accompanied Jim to Oaxaca, Mexico, on a medical mission trip. Fifteen miles from the nearest village, with no communication, the mule I was riding fell off a 25 foot cliff, leaving me with multiple fractures and in shock. After arriving home, I faced months in bed and a two year recuperation. Sleepless nights and ineffective pain medication became the norm. Jim took care of my every need.

As I struggled on my walker, Billy would quietly imitate

my labored shuffle, as I would attempt to get to the bathroom. When he wasn't at school, he would stay by my side in the bedroom and quietly play or read. Our little boy was compassionate beyond his years. Witnessing my near fatal accident affected Billy greatly.

My recuperation from a bilateral fractured pelvis and extensive nerve damage resulting from a sacral fracture left me unable to horseback ride, sit comfortably in a chair, climb stairs or walk with a quick stride. Cleaning a bathtub or vacuuming kicked up the nerve damage and made me feel like I was on fire. But I was fortunately able to continue my true love, downhill skiing. As long as I didn't have to 'pole' to get to a higher area, I did fine. Trading housework for snow skiing was no problem!

Constant pain interfered with so many physical activities that I once took for granite. I sold my horse. The golf clubs were put away for a time. Now that I couldn't participate in the upkeep of our home, Billy was now old enough to be Jim's helper. Their teamwork lasted only a short time before Billy's illness accelerated, leaving him physically exhausted. There was speculation from Dr. Colton that Billy was still trying to cope with my physical problems by creating his own.

My stepchildren, Lara and Jimmy, had a work ethic instilled in them from early childhood. They knew how to mow and weed-wack. Mucking stalls in the barn and putting hay in the loft for the horses were expected. Weekly chores were mandatory. Checking the oil on the car and changing a flat tire were taught prior to obtaining their driver's licenses. They both held part-time jobs while in high school.

Unlike his brother and sister, Billy rarely finished any physical labor he began. While riding the lawn mower or bringing in wood for the stove , he'd begin to yawn and linger in the kitchen. After eating handfuls of salty crackers and gulping down a drink, he would fall asleep on the couch. As Jim yelled for Billy to come outside to finish what he had started, I would proceed to make excuses for our son. "How is he ever going to learn basic skills in maintaining a home?" Jim asked in frustration. It was more of a statement than a question. In my heart I did not believe Billy was being defiant or lazy. Jim, however, was not so sure.

Jim's older children no longer lived at home. As both Billy and I became more physically needy, Jim's emotional separation from me was especially painful. When the stress in our home reached a boiling point, I would see him reading. Passing by, I would hear him snap a novel shut and mutter, "I can't even concentrate." He would head outside, rain or shine. Physical labor and landscaping allowed him hours of sorting out life's problems. I never envisioned how I would later associate Jim's bad moods and frustrations with several completed projects.

Our normal activities turned into complicated trials. Billy's absences from school simply scratched the recorded surface compared with his late arrivals. It was nearly impossible to get him moving when the sun came up. With no evidence of fever, his dad would awaken him and insist that he try to make it to school on time. But the minute Jim left for work, Billy would be back in bed, fast asleep. Jim's blood pressure would rise every evening as he watched Billy romp through the family room. I had to confess that it was true: he appeared healthy and energetic in the evenings. Jim felt that I caved in repeatedly to goals he was attempting to set for Billy.

Billy frequently asked me why his dad was angry at him. Rather than trying to explain his father's silence and glaring looks, I insisted that Billy talk to his dad. When the wall of silence was erected around my husband, he became unapproachable for days. But when Billy would confront him and say, "Dad, why are you so mad at me?" Jim always softened toward Billy. I decided to let Billy and his dad work out their own relationship. Unable to defuse the tension in our home, I didn't even want to try and help.

We had to repeatedly rethink family vacations. Too many trips required alternative planning because Billy wasn't well. The pressure mounted as we would fail to agree on a possible destination. Our social life stalled as well. All spontaneity dissolved over the years. Jim and I agreed on very little. In countless areas, our lives were losing their joy, as we tired of the endless discussions about Billy. We were miserable. Yet the property, the deck and the house sure did look nice.

As the stress mounted, it was Billy who would come to us at night and say, "Are we going to pray together?" Jim and I would drag ourselves into our bedroom, taking our usual places, while praying as a family. One of us might remain silent, unable to earnestly pray aloud. The frustration over the latest disagreement of Billy's care or predicament became a stumbling block. But we were always present before God. Usually we arrived out of obedience, sometimes out of guilt, but we were always aware that we were coming before our Lord at the throne of grace.

My prayer time with Billy began when he was an infant. As I nursed him, it was an opportunity quietly pray. When he became a toddler, Billy joined me in praying aloud and asked his dad to join us. Our two-year-old felt it made perfect sense to be together as a family while reading the Bible, too. Jim had been reading to Billy each evening from a children's Bible, just as he had done when Jimmy and Lara were younger. As Billy matured, I witnessed my little boy studying the Word of God or praying alone in his bedroom. Seeking the Lord in our lives was as natural as breathing in and out.

During some of our most difficult evenings after Billy became ill, I would become acutely aware of an ugly presence in our midst. Silently, I would pray for protection over our family, for I felt a spiritual battle in process. I visualized God's angels at our door and in every corner of our property. I held fast to the passage in the Bible: *Submit yourselves, then, to God. Resist the devil, and he will flee from you. Come near to God and he will come near to you. James 4:7-8*

Even though we agreed on very little, we were in total agreement in the priority of prayer in our home. Our family's time with Jesus was the one constant. Our Savior was obedient, even to the point of death on the cross. Therefore, our time with the Lord was never up for negotiation.

Chapter 12

Friendship

Chapter 12

Friendship

T he importance of faithful women in my life cannot be exaggerated. When a child is sick, everyone in the household handles their weariness differently. When my emotional tank was empty, it was unrealistic to expect my husband to meet my needs. He was grieving in his own way. I knew where to turn.

> **Philippians 4:5-7**
> *Let your gentleness be evident to all. The Lord is near. Do not be anxious about anything, but in everything, by prayer and petition, with thanksgiving, present your requests to God. And the peace of God, which transcends all understanding, will guard your hearts and your minds in Christ Jesus.*

The stress and anger in our home became unbearable as Billy's illness progressed. His health defined everyday conversations. My husband and I rarely spoke of anything but Billy's medical care, his academics and his lack of social life. Jim would no longer indulge me in further discussions about our son's past struggles. Speculation regarding his future was met with a wall of silence. We drew further apart. Our intimacy, our humor, any normal routine were things of the past.

I would have felt totally isolated had it not been for Susan and Dee. One year prior to my son's onset of symptoms, these two women approached me at our Community Bible Study class to ask me to be prayer partners with them. This was an unfamiliar concept to me. My first response was, "How much time will it take?" I hedged, wanting no part of this additional social obligation. My calendar was packed and one more pencil mark on my only day off work was out of the question. After very little consideration, I politely told them, "Thanks for asking, but no thanks."

But there was no getting away from the persistence of these women. In essence, they hounded me! A little irritated, I wondered if they believed that I didn't pray frequently enough. On the defensive, I reasoned that I prayed with my family every evening and at mealtime. I had a personal relationship with Christ. I just didn't see their point. Susan called and caught me in a good mood, asking me over for breakfast with Dee. Curious and truly enjoying their company, I thought, "Why not?" Breakfast was always my favorite meal of the day.

We had a great time together. Laughing, we progressed to catching up on the events of the past week. Transferring from Susan's kitchen to the living room, we settled in with steaming cups of warm coffee in hand. Our mood gradually changed from levity to reverence. We began to pray for our time together, our country, our husbands and their places of work. Lifting up our kids and their teachers into His care, I felt empowered by the Holy Spirit in simply asking for His mercies to be poured out from heaven above. In silence, a peace entered our space. There was no mistaking that these godly women had invited me to be a part of their very personal time, a time in which to call upon Jesus to enter every area of our lives.

Sometimes we felt rushed through our 30 minute prayer time. Over the next year, however, these minutes extended into an hour. If we couldn't get together, the telephone worked. We became very dependent on the encouragement of one another. The three of us had our share of physical problems. Our empathy for each other was apparent to outsiders, as well. Instead of interacting like women in our forties, we acted like elderly old friends, grabbing one another's arms for support. Whoever felt the best on any given day would hold open a door as two of us would hobble through. Dee was diagnosed with multiple sclerosis shortly after we met. Susan was in total denial about a chronic back problem that would land her in bed in terrible pain for weeks. My own chronic pain stemmed from my 'mule and cliff' accident that had occurred shortly after meeting Susan. The three of us understood each others' physical limitations, sensing one another's downhill slides before words were spoken.

Now my friends heard all that was weighing on my heart. I shared every detail of my own problems, yet Billy's declining health superceded my inclination into self absorption. I knew the reason my body was falling apart. Questions concerning Billy and my frustration with his doctor were mounting. My friends watched me break down in tears on several occasions, and I'm not a weepy person. The tug of war that was escalating between Jim and me began to seep into our conversations. At times I wondered, "Oh Lord, did I say too much?" They had not known my husband before the stress over Billy's health had begun to interpose itself on our lives. What must they think of him? I was about to find out what true friends say and do when the marriage of a friend is in trouble.

One day, terribly hurt and angry at Jim, I dreaded seeing my girlfriends walk through my back door. My emotions were raw, and I knew if I got started talking, I might say too much. Uncharacteristically quiet, there was no hiding my heart from Susan and Dee. Now their questions began in earnest. Cracking, I poured out the horrible details of the latest painful argument in our home. As hurtful words spewed from my mouth, I wanted them to hate Jim as much as I did. As I slouched in despair, Susan grabbed both of my hands and firmly declared, "Jim loves you so much, Karen." I was floored as she continued, "Billy is not well, and he just doesn't know what to do either." There was no condemnation in her eyes toward the man I truly loved. Her words defused my anger. Expecting judgment or criticism toward my husband was foolish.

So from that day forward, we prayed for absolute unity and healing in my marriage. My heavenly Father's desire was for my family to be healthy and whole. Truly, all divisiveness in our marriage was the work of the adversary. Acknowledging this fact brought us absolute conviction, as we prayed in one accord for victory in my marriage. With equally firm determination, we asked the Lord to send someone wise and compassionate, one only known to Him, to present a definitive diagnosis for my sick boy.

Susan and Dee faithfully prayed for my family for years to come. It was the sweetest offering from my friends. I imagine that deep down, though never with spoken words, they must have been terribly angry at Jim on that day. Had they reacted with disgust, giving me justification for my anger, I fear that my heart would have been hardened. Rather than feeding my sorrows and telling me what I expected to hear, God used these dear friends to fix my eyes on the Lord. Their godly wisdom and personal restraint helped bring beauty from the ashes of my pain.

I only wished they had known Jim before Billy became sick.

Chapter 13

Achievements

Chapter 13

Achievements

Sick children can feel terribly isolated. The most effective remedy to the loneliness which attends chronic illness is that precious time given by family and friends.

> **Hebrews 4:15-16**
> *For we do not have a high priest who is unable to sympathize with our weaknesses, but we have one who has been tempted in every way, just as we are-yet without sin. Let us then approach the throne of grace with confidence, so that we may receive mercy and find grace to help us in our time of need.*

Billy had obtained all the merit badges required to become an Eagle Scout. Dedicated adult leaders in his troop gave wise counsel that the boys should try to achieve Scouting's highest rank by the age of fifteen. The Scoutmaster observed that at sixteen, girls and cars seemed to stall the enthusiasm of even the most focused boys. So Billy's Eagle Scout project, the final requirement, was designed and approved by the troop committee prior to his fifteenth birthday. His plan was to construct a fish pond, complete with a waterfall, for Boyds Presbyterian Church. This peaceful addition overlooking the cemetery would be an area of quiet reflection for the parishioners and community alike. Momentum stalled, however, when Billy dropped out of high school, undergoing multiple medical tests to hopefully identify the root cause of his failing health.

He could barely drag himself to the weekly troop meetings due to his fragile physical condition. Everyone knew that Billy was facing a muscle biopsy and the results could be grievous. A number of his fellow scouts had a suggestion. They reminded Billy that the purpose of his project was to demonstrate leadership skills, so they initiated a plan. The boys sat down with our son and together devised a rigorous work schedule for themselves over the two weekends prior to his surgery. Billy's role would be to supervise. Word went out and help arrived from his troop, his church youth group and kids from his high school. These boys and their parents gave of their time and energy for a greater purpose. They succeeded in completing a stunning pond for the enjoyment of our community and in support of a boy who loved scouting.

Three months later, his Eagle Scout ceremony was underway, with over one hundred guests in attendance. Friends and family came from out of town for his big event. My parents took the auto train from Florida to share in their grandson's momentous day. Even my sister's son, Michael, came from Connecticut to support his cousin. Barely able to stand at the altar, Billy's shoulders were slumped. His emaciated frame looked out of place among his fellow healthy scouts. We had a long day ahead of us. I wondered how he would possibly hold up?

It was time for Billy's scout master, Bob Hernandez, to take a moment and share his recollections of Billy's scouting history. As Bob began to speak, he lost his composure. My heart stopped. A wave of emotional distress rippled through the sanctuary. Billy averted his eyes, looking down at the floor. Finally I caught his attention. Grinning at one another, I prayed he was reading my mind, "Bob is so big hearted, Billy. He cries at every one of his boys Eagle Scout ceremonies!" Everyone took a deep breath as Bob regained his composure, completing his many generous accolades of Billy's scouting days.

At the conclusion of the ceremony, Billy was exhausted. He accepted countless hugs and congratulatory handshakes before moving on to the church social hall. Scouts and their parents feasted on several six-foot subs. Actually, they deserved surf and turf for their dedication. I felt such pride, watching so many decent young men gather in one place. I wondered how aware they might be that each had actually *loved* their friend into his present accomplishment. As they laughed and horsed around, I scanned the room, looking for my Eagle Scout.

I finally found him. In a distant corner of the room I saw my dad, Billy's namesake, sitting beside his grandson. Bill Du Bois had his arm around Billy Rhea. They both looked worn out. Even so, each broke into a broad smile and their shoulders bounced up and down as they began to laugh out loud. This was an identical characteristic they shared, along with being left-handed and color-blind. No one humored Billy like his Pop.

Little did I know that while Billy was in a battle for his life, my father was fighting his own war with undiagnosed ALS, Lou Gehrig's Disease. Looking back, it was truly a gift from God that brought Billy and his Pop to this special moment that day. It would be my dad's last trip to Maryland. In the arms of my father and surrounded by so many loyal friends and role models, Billy's deteriorating health did not define his day. Everyone's presence and joy with one another proclaimed, "Billy, you're loved and you are the best."

Chapter 14

"Am I Dying?"

Chapter 14

"Am I Dying?"

~~~

Has God abandoned us? How can a loving God allow little ones to suffer?

1 Peter 5:10
And the God of all grace, who called you to his eternal glory in Christ, after you have suffered a little while, will himself restore you and make you strong, firm and steadfast.

Sitting on the floor by Billy's bed, I gently ran my fingers over his forehead and through his thick, wavy hair. His eyes were once again puffy and his lids were heavy. "Mom, do you think I will live long enough to get my driver's license?" The tightening in my throat arrested any wise response I tried to muster up. "Are you feeling terrible today, Buddy?" My voice cracked. Seeing the tears welling up in my eyes, he assured me, "Yes, but I bet I'll feel better tomorrow." We talked for a while and agreed that God gives some people bodies that last ninety-nine years and others very little time at all. We acknowledged that only He knows the hour when we will each be in His presence.

"Mom, remember what Pastor Dale said?" Turning around to the headboard that doubled as a book shelf, he began pulling out the notes he had taken during a sermon just a few weeks earlier. Discovering the reference for which he was searching, Billy pointed out that when Jesus wept at the death of his friend Lazarus, he cried the very tears of God. He continued, "Mom, He truly is the author of life, not death." My son's faith and assurance of Christ's love in the midst of his miserable physical state was firmly established in his heart. Recollecting our pastor's sermon helped to assure me that Jesus was indeed grieved by my son's failing health.

The Great Physician's timing made no sense to me at all. My praying and pleading produced a continuous string of questions, rather than the answers I wanted. "Wait," became the response I learned to expect from my Lord. I wanted to believe that a diagnosis, even a miracle, was around the corner. These years in the wilderness were taking their toll.

Sometimes I would sit at the dinner table and stare into my husband's eyes. He may as well have been in another room. Then I would fix my gaze on Billy. How could Jim be so cold to us? How could he not see an illness stirring in our son? As I prepared myself for any diagnosis, Jim firmly believed the doctors were heading in the wrong direction. He became adamantly opposed to the surgeon preforming a muscle biopsy on Billy's thigh. He felt it was unnecessary. Elevated CPK levels from blood test results indicated there was stress on Billy's muscles and heart. This was where the notion evolved, pointing to mitochondrial disease. This deadly disease would cause a fatal cellular breakdown in the body. The results from a muscle biopsy held the answer. After doing a bit of research of his own, Jim told me that

Billy's somewhat elevated CPK levels did not warrant this invasive procedure. He repeated his belief right up to the time of the procedure. "I don't want them cutting into my son's thigh." Furious, I would think, but never verbally express, " Do you have any better ideas?"

Through Billy's travails, I did spend more time with my Lord than I ever had previously. Bringing His children unto Himself was always the Lord's ultimate desire. Well, God had my attention. I longed to experience His mercy and grace. Some days I had glimmers of hope. Yet most were filled with anger and despair.

Little did I know that our grievous circumstances reached far beyond my immediate family. Billy's physical and mental deterioration were gaining the attention of countless skeptics. If I heard it once, I heard it a hundred times, "Why would God allow your family to go through this nightmare?" There was no doubt in my mind that our present circumstances were not of my Lord's making. The Prince of Darkness lurked somewhere amidst the desolation. I always knew that God was a God of order, not confusion. I did feel terribly lonely but never alone. Each time I rose after being on my knees in prayer, I would stand weary, but refreshed. Only the Holy Spirit could renew my spirit in such grief. My prayers were anything but eloquent. I prayed specifically, "Lord, if it be your will, please let Billy get his driver's license."

Chapter 15

Blinded Men

Chapter 15

Blinded Men

The answer I had been awaiting yet dreading was just hours away. Billy was having a good day, so I believed that whatever illness would be identified must be treatable.

> **Isaiah 59:14**
> *So justice is driven back, and righteousness stands at a distance; truth has stumbled in the streets, honesty cannot enter.*

Jim and I sat with Billy in the neurologist's conference room. We spoke not a word. Watching the clock, I marveled how these past ten minutes could feel longer than the past two months. Suddenly the door swung open and the doctor entered and sat down. Not uttering a word, he flipped open a thick folder with William Joel Rhea written boldly on the front, and my heart began to race. Reaching over, I put my arm around my son's shoulder.

With no emotion, the doctor stated that Billy's EMG and EEG were a little off, but there was nothing to be alarmed about. Then he mechanically flipped through page after page and announced, "There is no evidence of mitochondrial disease or muscular dystrophy." Continuing, he flatly stated, "In fact, there is nothing wrong with your son." I was stunned.

I said, "Wait a minute! He was in the hospital for three days last month with his kidneys shutting down." Leaning back in his chair, the doctor snapped Billy's folder closed and announced, "Your son is not sick." Rudely he added that if I really wanted to see a sick kid, I should walk down the halls of his pediatric hospital. He turned to my husband, Jim, and sternly said, "I suggest you get psychological counseling for your son and your wife." Before he walked out the door, he shook Billy's hand and, forcing a fake smile, he said, "Have a wonderful, healthy life, Billy."

Jim glared at me. Already suspicious that I had developed a growing neurosis concerning our son's medical conditions, the test results confirmed the theory that had been implanted years ago by Billy's previous physician. Jim now had the confirmation to support this idea that, somehow, through too much attention and over-protection, I had been making Billy ill.

Leaving the hospital, Jim was leading the way to the car. Looking back at me he snapped, "I did not want them cutting into Billy's thigh. Are you happy now?" All I could think was, "Happy? Happy?" I couldn't remember when I last felt happy. Nobody, not the surgeon, not his pediatrician, not Jim would discuss Billy's three day hospitalization just one month ago. Where they all blind? Weary, I started to wonder if I was crazy. Now I began to doubt myself.

My morning had begun in hopeful anticipation, but now I was rocked with confusion and grief.

I didn't think our lives could get any worse. But I was wrong.

Chapter 16

Deception Versus Light

Chapter 16

Deception Versus Light

For six months Billy struggled to fake an appearance of being healthy. I pulled away from him, in an attempt to not pamper him. According to his highly respected neurologist, my strong desire to nurture him in illness was accentuating his symptoms. Oddly enough, as I distanced myself from Billy, he continued to become worse. What now?

> **Galatians 5:7-8**
> *You were running a good race. Who cut in on you and kept you from obeying the truth? That kind of persuasion does not come from the one who calls you.*

Billy yelled out as he swallowed his soup. "Oh no, something is happening!" After acquiring a rigid stance, he stated unequivocally that he felt numb on one entire side of his body. Fifteen minutes later, he said the other side was affected. His left hand did appear rigid. His tongue was visibly swelling. Like countless time before, I dove for the

Benadryl. An hour later these weird symptoms began to subside. It was time for us to meet our friends, Mac and Harriet, at a restaurant, for we were the decoy for Harriet's surprise 50th birthday party at their home later that evening. Billy was invited as well. Instead he headed to his bedroom and said, "I don't feel well. Have a good time Mom and Dad."

After being seated at the restaurant with our friends and their son, Jim apologized that Billy hadn't joined us. "He's a *little* sick again." As he was pressed for more details, Jim changed the subject. I knew he couldn't stand to spend one more moment discussing Billy's health. This was always how Jim *managed* his anger. Clamming up, he changed the subject. Leaving the room was a little more difficult, as he was stuck in a restaurant. Yet being with good friends helped defuse the tension between Jim and me.

After our meal we drove to Mac and Harriet's home on Sugarloaf Mountain in Adamstown, Maryland. Their steep driveway packed with hairpin turns gave Jim the opportunity to use the four wheel drive on the Jeep. The drop offs made the palms of my hands sweat, so I simply kept my eyes shut. Laughing as we got out of the car, we entertained a few fatal possibilities if someone with poor judgment was behind the wheel. Entering the house, a delightful group of people made the hours fly by. A harpist entertained the guests. The evening was relaxing and elegant. But I began to watch the clock, telling Jim I wanted to get home to Billy. Therefore, we were one of the first couples to leave.

Returning home, Jim's newfound icy silence exploded. He observed that every time we planned to go out together, Billy would stage some dramatic episode. This declaration began the harshest, ugliest exchange of words in our 18 years of marriage. All our hurt and hate had truly opened the gates of Hell. My recent complacency and self doubt toward Billy's unknown condition came to an abrupt halt. I could not prove a thing, but I would not give up. I knew in my heart that the doctors, Jim, friends and teachers were all wrong, dead wrong. Sitting passively by would no longer continue. Maybe I was looking in the wrong direction.

Could something in our home be making Billy sick? After speaking with our county's Environmental Protection Department, I learned that decades earlier, evidence uncovered high levels of nitrates in our town. So I decided to hire a scientific research company to test our well water for bacteria and nitrates. Two weeks after the technician took away samples from our well, the results and the invoice for payment arrived. The results revealed that our water samples met the Federal and State Safe Drinking Water Act. Jim believed we were flushing hundreds of dollars down the toilet. His opinion mattered little to me. I felt compelled to search for the truth.

Billy had a regular physical scheduled with his pediatrician on his sixteenth birthday. Prior to the appointed date, I fired off another letter to his doctor, articulating the severity of my son's new symptoms. I added that the pain from his swollen toes and fingers were bringing Billy to my bedside in the middle of the night, over and over again. He had five urinary tract infections in the past year alone. Once again I reminded him of the three-day dehydration that landed him in the hospital eight months earlier. I ended my letter with, "I look forward to hearing what you think." I dropped it in the mail.

Jim was trying to defuse our present marriage crisis. He asked if I would go with him to a jungle resort in Belize for some rest and relaxation. After all, a friend could stay at the house and watch Billy. Following all the ugly things he said to me, I told him to take someone else. I was totally confused as to why he wanted to take me away with him. Nothing sounded worse.

Jim wouldn't let up. He pleaded with me, adding that he

really did love me. I wasn't buying it. Wanting to get him off my back, I told him I would give him an answer after Billy's check up the following week. I Believed that Dr. Witmer would recognize the significance of these new problems and I focused only on the upcoming appointment on February 2nd. Another unexpected blow was approaching.

After Billy's appointment, Dr. Witmer declared, "He's a little underweight, but otherwise he is just fine." As Billy shuffled to the waiting room, I quietly spoke to his doctor in the hallway. Asking if he read my letter, this trusted pediatrician formed the same distant, "Don't start this again" glaze in his eye that I had learned to read so well from Dr. Colton. A chill went up my spine. Getting nowhere, I told him of my husband's desire to take me out of the country. Dr. Witmer agreed that it would be ideal for the two of us to get away without Billy for a short break.

The following week I prayed and cried out to God. For the first time I was in a battle with my Lord. I hated everything around me, except for my son. I could trust no one. I felt isolated and rejected. In desperation, I told God that I was leaving Jim, or I prayed that he would leave me. I would not go away with him. All the resentment, hurt and anger I harbored was a recipe for failure. Tucking my knees up to my chest, I wrapped my arms around my legs and rocked back and forth. In the fetal position, I fell asleep. A voice caused my eyes to spring open. Sitting up straight, I heard, "Be obedient unto Me and go with Jim."

Now I am very strong-willed. But at that instant I relinquished as Jesus instructed me to obey Him and go. Reluctantly, I began to make our travel arrangements. As I called the airlines, I looked up the jungle resort on the internet. My eyes feasted on the pictures of rustic huts, wild cats and monkeys. The anticipation of this vacation became as sweet as walking into my favorite ice cream store and purchasing German chocolate cake ice cream in a waffle cone. My heavenly Father was directing me in this endeavor.

Jim had the opportunity to stay at this resort two years earlier. Following one of his short term medical mission trips in Belize, the missionary from the area planned a final day of reflection at the resort. Jim wanted to show me this tropical wonderland. The hardest job would be telling Billy that we were going away. As I delicately explained where we were going, he simply shrugged his shoulders and said, "It sounds like fun."

At the end of February 2000, through obedience to God, I sat next to my husband as the plane lifted off the tarmac at Dulles International Airport. I was now actually looking forward to our vacation in sunny Belize.

Chapter 17

Preparation

Chapter 17

Preparation

In quiet prayer, I spent years telling God what I desired. Now I began to comprehend the difficult art of listening. God had told me what He required of me. Blessings do come in unusual ways.

> **James 1:19-20**
> *My dear brothers, take note of this: everyone should be quick to listen, slow to speak and slow to become angry, for man's anger does not bring about the righteous life that God desires.*

Standing in the jungle compound of Banana Bank with Jim, I soaked in its beauty. The echo of parrots, mingled with the chatter of wild monkeys filled the air. A sizeable primate scampered deftly across a rooftop to peer down at us. Leaning over, I repeatedly zipped and unzipped that zipper which altered my pants into shorts. Now I had the monkey's attention. Within minutes, he was putty in my hands. Grabbing my hand in his, he placed his tail firmly around my arm to walk with me. Yes, the monkey and I had a thing going, and Jim snapped enough photographs to prove its validity to the folks back home!

Our week away was nothing less than magical. Jim and I had placed ourselves in a completely different world. We fell in love once again. I had not seen my husband look tenderly at me in ages. We took note that the owners of Banana Bank were believers and always surrounded their guests with prayer. Wrapped in this peaceful environment, discussions about Billy's present situation and even his questionable future became calm. We called Billy twice. Over the phone his voice sounded flat, but I assured him that we would be home on Sunday night. "Love you Mom. I love you too, Billy."

After lunch on Saturday, Jim and I were just returning from an enjoyable outing. Suddenly an overwhelming feeling of panic gripped me. I had to get back and call home. Two calls produced nothing except my own voice on our home answering machine. I wondered where Billy must be. A man walked into the hotel lobby and said, "Mrs. Rhea, you need to call the hospital in the United States."

My body trembled as an emergency room physician declared, "Get home now if you want to see your son alive; tomorrow will be too late." He suspected a brain aneurysm. I gave permission for the hospital to perform a spinal tap. Over the next two hours, our desperate attempts to get a flight home early were failing. The only plane to the United States from this remote area was filled. I called my parents in Florida. The emergency room had contacted them earlier that afternoon. As the doctor explained Billy's grave condition to my Dad, he could hear Billy screaming in the background. Our inability to get home and Billy's desperate cries of anguish left us terribly helpless. We wept. Finally, Jim and I went into our room and prayed for Billy. We were in total accord; unified as one. "Please, Father God, we need to get home."

After speaking with the doctor in the hospital, a representative from the airlines finally agreed to reserve us their only remaining seats in 1st class on the only flight leaving Belize to the United States. Every complicated travel detail, as well as the airline transfers through Texas, were in God's hands. Yet I had no peace. Billy was alone.

What was I doing on this airplane? How could I have left him? Thinking back four years earlier to Lara and Alan's wedding, I remembered my promise to never leave Billy alone and helpless again. What had I done? I prayed like a broken record, "Please Father, let him live; let him live; let him live." It was the longest ten hours of my life.

Chapter 18

Anticipation

Chapter 18

Anticipation

I can't believe this is happening. Please God, let it be me and not my child.

Psalm 42: 1-3
As the deer pants for streams of water, so my soul pants for you, O God. My soul thirsts for God, for the living God. When can I go and meet with God? My tears have been my food day and night, while men say to me all day long, "Where is your God?"

Panic swelled in my heart. How long had I been sitting in my car, lost in deep thought, while my son lay dying in the ICU? Turning off the ignition, I gathered up my overnight bag and my purse running back to the entrance to the hospital.

In a surreal, dreamlike state, I found myself alone in the elevator. Struggling to steady my finger, I pressed three, feeling an urgency to get back to the pediatric ICU. As the doors closed, I collapsed, crying aloud. The elevator seemed to rise in slow motion. An audible, reassuring voice said, "I've given her the answer." Jumping to my feet, my mind now began to race. I searched the confines of the elevator, knowing not another soul was present.

What was that obscure disease mentioned by a female doctor earlier that morning? Where was she at this moment? As the elevator doors opened, I recognized her coming down the hall toward me, carried along by a determined stride. "Please, can I have just one minute of your time?" As I stepped off the elevator, she breezed past me. I found her standing where I had been a moment before. As the doors began to shut, she momentarily held her hand against the closing doors. With a grin and a wave of her hand, she sang out, "Sorry, not right now Mrs. Rhea, I'm late for church! I'll be back later." I now remembered. It was Sunday morning.

Rushing on to Billy's room, I found him under close watch by Jim and a nurse. I riffled through my bag to retrieve my Bible. Flipping it open, a passage from John 11 virtually leapt off the pages. *Jesus said, "This sickness will not end in death. No, it is for God's glory so that God's Son may be glorified through it."*

At that very moment I knew this was not the end of Billy's life. Even in my exhausted state, I smiled, knowing that God had tossed me two precious reminders that He was in complete control. Praying with great anticipation, I felt an excitement that if expressed outwardly would have been mistaken for total lunacy.

I now felt perfectly alert, despite all the stress and my lack of sleep. Countless questions entered my mind. I had waited for years for God to send someone to diagnose my son. Now the wait was coming to an end. I looked at my critically ill boy. Leaning down, I whispered in his ear, "Hang on Buddy, we're praying for you."

Jim and I commandeered opposite sides of Billy's

hospital bed and quietly talked about things of little importance, yet none the less, necessary. "Is there anyone else we should call? Are the dogs inside the house or in the back yard? Should we cancel patients this week?" At this point there was little else left to say regarding Billy's condition. We did have a new found comfort in being by his side, which softened the horror of his critical condition. I wanted to believe that our physical presence now protected our son from any further harm. Jim and I kept expecting Billy to suddenly wake up and join in our conversation. Instead, the constant ticking, whistling, and beeping of the malfunctioning medical equipment provided the reminder that neither modern medicine nor Jim's and my love would be Billy's salvation. Only God was in control.

At least we were no longer on an airplane, unable to hold Billy's hand. His nurse pulled up a chair. Sitting down, she shared the details of Billy's arrival in the emergency room the previous afternoon. I longed to know everything.

Chapter 19

Servants of God

Chapter 19

Servants of God

The events that led to our present Sunday morning unfolded. It was all too perfect to have any other signature but the inscription of my Lord.

> **Isaiah 54:17**
> *No weapon forged against you will prevail, and you will refute every tongue that accuses you. This is the heritage of the servants of the Lord, and this is their vindication from me, declares the Lord.*

Billy's pediatrician, Dr. Witmer, arrived at the hospital emergency room to inform the medical staff of our son's lengthy, troubling history. Even though he wasn't on call, he felt compelled to physically stay by Billy's side and assist in any way possible. As blood was drawn to check for drug use, this good doctor assured them that the results would be negative. In an instant, Billy went from being somewhat coherent to screaming and thrashing for hours. Dr. Witmer and our friend Merhnoosh stayed with Billy into the early hours of the following morning, until Jim and I arrived at the hospital. Mehrnoosh never left his side.

As Jim and I were desperately trying to get home from Belize on Saturday night, arrangements were being made to admit Billy to the Intensive Care Unit. The emergency room was understaffed with orderlies. So a physician and nurse from the ICU volunteered to transport Billy back upstairs to the pediatric ICU where they worked. In the elevator, June Harris, R.N. recalled having an instructor in nursing school who had Billy's identical bronze skin tone. This particular rare disease, left untreated, would lead to a potentially fatal, physical crisis. Listening to her insight, the critical care physician began to research the defining criteria of Addison's Disease.

Now, less than 24 hours after Billy's friend, Lyndsay, called an ambulance, Jim and I listened intently as the nurse carefully explained the symptoms which transpire during an Addisonian crisis. She described the physical breakdown that occurs when the adrenal glands do not produce hydrocortisone. Basically, all the electrolytes in the brain short circuit, and the patient is rendered helpless by confusion, combativeness and unconsciousness. The majority of crisis patients die, resulting in a definitive diagnosis, only revealed at autopsy.

We learned the adrenal glands are known as the fight-or-flight glands. Their main function is to control various forms of stress in the body. When the body is under physical or mental stress, the adrenal glands produce increased amounts of hydrocortisone. This natural steroid is critical in controlling blood pressure, hydration, inflammation, mental cognizance and the ability to fight infection.

When the adrenal glands shut down, the pituitary gland tries to compensate by working overtime, in the process producing an excess of melanin. Melanin, which is responsible for skin pigmentation, turned Billy's skin a deep bronze color. He had lived so long with undiagnosed Addison's that he developed problems which had never previously been associated with this disease. Fatigue, body aches, recurrent infections, salt cravings, dehydration and a bronze skin tone are known symptoms of adrenal insufficiency. But dilating eyes, slurred speech and swollen face, fingers and toes were variables previously not associated with this disease. Billy's past symptoms were beginning to make sense.

As a last ditch effort to save his life, his body was flooded with intravenous hydrocortisone. It would take 48 to 96 hours to confirm a diagnosis. We could not wait for this confirmation, for if her suspicions of Addison's were wrong, the hydrocortisone would not have any long-lasting, adverse effects. It would take just as long for our son to regain consciousness, if he were to respond and awaken at all. His attending nurse pleaded faintly, "If you are people who pray, do so now." My husband and I were way ahead of her. Jim and I called family and friends, passing the telephone receiver back and forth, repeating over and over again the events of the past 24 hours. With that, the word spread. "Billy Rhea needs your prayers."

The very hand of God positioned the final pieces of our six-year puzzle. My long awaited prayer for someone to diagnose my son was being answered affirmatively. I now understood that even Dr. Witmer had been used in a very unique way. When this good doctor encouraged me to leave for Belize with Jim, I was removed from the picture. Deep down I knew that if Billy had been under my watchful eye on the afternoon of his downward spiral, Jim and the doctors would have repeated their condemnation toward my perception of urgency toward his care. Removed from my son's side, I was no longer under their critical microscope. Only in my absence was their undivided attention placed on Billy; where it should have been, all along.

Chapter 20

Called To This Very Moment

Chapter 20

Called To This Very Moment

God now had everyone's attention. Doubts, mistrust and arrogance were finally silenced.

James 5:14
Is any one of you sick? He should call the elders of the church to pray over him and anoint him with oil in the name of the Lord.

The hospital hallway outside of Billy's room was reminiscent of the depressive atmosphere to be found in a funeral home. Because only two people at a time were permitted in the intensive care rooms, Jim and I were constantly stepping outside, making room for the next visitor to enter and view my son. His unresponsiveness coupled with his pale and emaciated appearance shocked family and friends alike. The downcast countenance on every face reminded me of those sympathetic expressions following my sister's murder in 1983, those same looks, seared into my memory, that I wished never to see again.

Pastors Dale and Steve from our church entered the room. The nurse stood her ground, "Two of you will have to leave." Pastor Dale stood on equally firm footing. "The four of us are going to anoint this boy with oil and pray for healing." He invited her to join us, but she would need to give us a few minutes. She exited the room.

From his coat pocket, our senior pastor drew forth a small jar of oil. With heartfelt empathy Pastor Dale turned to me and said, "You were right all along." Terribly hurt, I wanted to hear those exact words from everyone. But there was no satisfaction in my seemingly brilliant perception of Billy's fragile state. Presently the four of us were called to this very moment.

We positioned ourselves around my son's bed. Praying in one accord, warmth spread through my body, filling me from head to toe. How odd that I couldn't close my eyes. I was fixed on every action involving my son. Jim held Billy's hand. I took note of the tender expressions of deep love and concern as our pastors called on the Holy Spirit and the healing power of our Great Physician, Jesus. As Pastor Dale touched my son's head with oil, Jim suddenly jumped. "Billy just squeezed my hand! Do you know where you are, Buddy?" Billy shook his head yes. I couldn't move. Jim leaned close to Billy's ear. "Do you know who is here with you?" Billy whispered, "My pastors."

I recalled those words written by the apostle John that I had read that very morning. *"This sickness will not end in death. No it is for God's glory so that God's Son may be glorified through it."* Closing my eyes, the glorious words of the old hymn filled my heart; *On Christ the solid rock I stand, all other ground is sinking sand*.....and I thanked my Father in heaven for His abounding mercy and grace. What a glorious March day it had turned out to be. Springtime had arrived.

Chapter 21

Trust Abandoned

Chapter 21

Trust Abandoned

Repentance is hard to achieve when anger dims all reason and recognition. I wanted the human conditions of pride and arrogance to be laid bare. My trust in overly confident people, especially physicians, would be slow to return.

Romans 12:2
Do not conform any longer to the pattern of this world, but be transformed by the renewing of your mind. Then you will be able to test and approve what God's will is- his good, pleasing and perfect will.

After Billy was transferred out of the ICU into the pediatric ward, I took a long look into my son's eyes and could not fight back my own tears. The whites of his eyes had been dull for so long and his irises so grey that I had been unaware of their gradual decline. Following five days of hydrocortisone treatment, his beautiful blue eyes were now restored. They glistened radiantly, as if he was once again ten years old.

As I pointed out this exciting change to Jim, there was an abrupt knock on the door of Billy's hospital room. Robbed of the beauty of that moment, a face peered around the slightly cracked door. I immediately recognized the doctor who had curtly dismissed us eight months earlier after the results of my son's muscle biopsy proved normal. "May I please come in?" Jim was gracious and invited him to join us. I was too incensed to say a word.

His face carried a pained expression that appeared genuine. I felt as if we were in the middle of a dramatic stage production, and the next actor had just come into view of the audience. I thought, "Oh, this guy is good." Apologizing over and over again, he acknowledged his own ugly words from months ago, repeating, "If you want to see a sick child, you should walk down the halls of this hospital." My mind raced back and forth in confusion. What was he doing here? The doctor explained that he had chosen pediatric neurology because he simply loved children. He then asked to speak with Billy. Emotionally choking on his words, he said, "Billy, if I could turn back the clock to that July day in my office and if I had taken a deeper look......if only I had referred you to an endocrinologist. I'm so sorry." Billy stared at him with a puzzled look and declared, "That's okay, I'm feeling better now that I'm taking medication."

He excused himself from the room as he repeated, "I'm so sorry." I don't think he was quite out of ear shot when I announced, "Well, he's hoping to avoid litigation!" Jim corrected me. "Can't you see that man is truly sorry? This is not even the hospital where he has privileges." The doctor had traveled across town just to meet with Billy, yet I would need to digest Jim's words over time, before I would reconsider my view and accept this doctor's genuine apology.

One week after descending into an acute Addisonian crisis, Billy was discharged from the hospital. After saying his farewells to the nurses and doctors in the Pediatric ICU, we gathered up his 'overnight' bag, flowers, balloons, countless gifts, goodies and get well cards. Our son had a new bounce in his step, and his smile beamed, expressing pure joy as he left the hospital. Suddenly he stopped, turning to face his dad with a deeply serious expression, "Is this what it feels like to be awake?" Embracing Billy while attempting to hide his emotions, Jim sputtered, "I guess so." As we continued our walk to the car, his stride quickened, transforming into a skip down the sidewalk. Shouting back to us and flashing a handsome smile, he declared, "Mom, Dad, imagine all I need is a few pills a day to feel this great!" Once again, this was my "Sweet William."

Chapter 22

Revenge to Restoration

Chapter 22

Revenge to Restoration

When my son's six year plight ended, his miraculous survival of an Addisonian crisis consumed my thoughts. Rather than exhibiting joy and delight, I wore my anger like a crown. I plotted day and night against those whose ignorance had contributed to Billy's lost adolescence. Every participant who had a part in stealing away his precious years would pay.

> **James 3:9-11**
> *With the tongue we praise our Lord and Father, and with it we curse men, who have been made in God's likeness. Out of the same mouth come praise and cursing. My brothers, this should not be. Can both fresh water and salt water flow from the same spring?*

I grabbed every opportunity to tell anyone who would listen of Billy's years of distress, pointing out that his illness was very real indeed. How dare these physicians suggest Billy was making himself sick with some psychological mumbo-jumbo. Accusing me of contributing to my son's declining health, their incompetence would come back to haunt them all. These so-called doctors had been dead wrong all along. Had any one of them looked at his hormonal levels through the appropriate blood test, coupled with a 24-hour urine catch, the answer would have been discovered years earlier. I felt vindication as each and every listener expressed their own outrage at the medical community.

At home, my son wouldn't allow me unlimited liberty in voicing my outrage. Billy always reminded me of the facts. Addison's Disease affects one in one hundred thousand adults. There were no statistics in children in March 2000. "It's rare mom!" He would add, "If I have to have a rare disease, this was the one to have." Oral medication, morning and night, controlled his adrenal insufficiency. Billy would now wear a medical ID tag for those "fight or flight" situations. A physical injury, surgery or even mental stress could throw him into another life threatening crisis. Also, a stomach virus would demand immediate IV saline and hydrocortisone. But his endocrinologist projected a good future and a normal life span for Billy.

I believed Billy's optimism would naturally waver as he attempted to regain momentum in his life. How could any child lose so many critical years of adolescent development and not be adversely affected? Certainly those past years of condemnation would need to be addressed in the future. After collecting the mounds of Billy's hospital and physician's records, I consulted an attorney. I was informed that my only chance of successful litigation would be to take *every* doctor that *ever* cared for Billy and press charges of medical negligence. I was not willing to do this.

Only Dr. Colton and the emergency room doctor who dismissed Billy with a 'sinus infection' one year earlier had been terribly negligent. Even though Dr. Witmer had missed the mark during the past year, referrals to specialists were quickly given to me. Their private practice had been genuinely supportive. Basically, I didn't have a case. Billy had lived. That was the long and the short of it. Even though significant mistakes had been made, not every doctor was at fault.

Yes, there was enough blame to go around. Besides the doctors, there were certain teachers and administrators who had belittled my son. Also, words of friends and family who questioned my parenting skills echoed relentlessly in my head. These detestable thoughts haunted my innermost being. I felt those lost years of Billy's precious childhood could have been avoided had anyone listened to me. My outrage deepened. I no longer slept. I withdrew and felt completely and utterly alone.

One Sunday morning in July, our family was in church singing a hymn. I was so angry that I couldn't stand, much less sing. Exhausted, I fought back the tears. I just couldn't continue with my destructive mentality anymore. Silently I begged God to take away the hate I was so deeply feeling. Leaving the sanctuary, I sensed a sweetness that I had not felt since Billy had awakened in the intensive care unit four months earlier. When I asked for His forgiveness as I brought my hateful pride before His throne, Jesus reminded me that I had been forgiven on the cross a long time ago.

Chapter 23

Settling In

Chapter 23

Settling In

A word or facial expression could trigger my mind into a destructive rehashing of conversations and situations that occurred years ago. Would I ever move beyond this pitiful tendency?

Psalm 30:5
For his anger lasts only a moment, but his favor lasts a lifetime; weeping may remain for a night, but rejoicing comes in the morning.

Yes, it was time to lay down my anger and forgive. Truly, it wasn't that easy. Often, I felt very self-righteous, even justified in my outrage; I would dwell there for days. But that unsettling weariness would return, reminding me that it was time to once again lay down my anger at the foot of the cross. Sometimes I needed to repent of my anger several times a day. At times, I failed miserably as fury crept into my mind. Even years later, a difficult day would make me believe that I had made no progress at all. Yet in prayer, I was always reminded that Satan delighted in robbing me of my joy. In my mind I refused to give him a foothold. "Get behind me Satan," became my battle cry, for the victory was always in Jesus.

The most amazing transformation happened. Early one morning while I was praying, Billy's physician, Dr.Colton, came to mind. For once, I was not listing all of his mistakes as he treated my boy for many years as his health declined. In a conversation with my Lord, I wondered how this man's heart regarded the entire matter of Billy Rhea? Living in a small town, I believed he must have known of Billy's continued deterioration after we left his care. At that instant, my memories flashed to countless encounters with this doctor. His care on most days proved kind and excellent. Once, Dr. Colton even stayed after hours to expertly suture a facial laceration after Billy took a nose dive off a kitchen chair. Passing us off to the emergency room was never a consideration. Touching on past memories such as these helped to erase the horns and devil's tail that I had associated with this man. He simply failed to keep watch at a critical juncture, unaware of the danger that lay ahead.

Now, Christ showed me how He must have felt, as His disciples fell asleep one by one in the Garden of Gethsemane. Overwhelmed by sorrow as to His coming crucifixion, those closest to Him neglected to keep watch and pray. They, too, were unaware. Yet, He forgave each and every one. This realization allowed blessings to flow unrestrained into my life.

Forgiveness toward Jim came easily. He was terribly hard on himself as he reflected on his misguided opinions of Billy. I was quite concerned about Jim's inability to forgive himself. Yet once our son returned to school and became involved in numerous activities, Jim's tendency to beat himself up emotionally eased. Billy's happiness was infectious. My marriage with Jim was restored. Together we shared a renewed intimacy and mutual respect for each other. Our humor helped tip the previously weighted scales of sullen drudgery to sweet levity.

The dark cloud that had settled over our home for too many years dissipated. The man I fell in love with decades ago was back.

Chapter 24

A Season of Adjusting

Chapter 24

A Season of Adjusting

Letting go and learning to be simply, mom rather than caretaker and advocate, has been a journey.

Psalm 34:4
I sought the Lord, and he answered me; he delivered me from all my fears.

In high school, Billy became Bill. Getting back into the groove of public school was a challenge. His enthusiasm for every subject and his over-involvement in countless extra-curricular activities was creating a difficult balancing act. Jim and I hated to say no to his mounting schedule. We knew he would have to learn a few things the hard way. Often he would become overly tired or upset, winding up sick for days on end. Since he missed a year of school, he felt disconnected with kids in his grade, seeing them as immature.

Bill had to repeat 9th grade. Even though he opted to attend summer school to try and catch up quickly, he needed certain credits that left him no option but to stay back a year. He was at least one or two years older than his classmates. Certainly he had been through something that most adults never survive. He gravitated toward students who were mature and focused. Bill fumed as he witnessed disrespectful students in the classroom, especially in the presence of the teachers he admired . He grew unsympathetic as he became aware of kids experimenting with drugs or drinking. He felt the popular slogan, "Friends don't let friends drive drunk," should be changed to "Friends don't have friends that get drunk." He would say, "They ought to feel out of control for years and have no choices and then maybe they wouldn't waste their lives." My son was becoming angry, rather than compassionate. The joy was slipping away.

Exactly one year following his diagnosis, during his junior year, the pressures in Bill's life began crashing down on him. As his friends were getting ready to graduate, Bill was facing an added year of high school. Terribly depressed, he began to spend more time alone. For so many years Bill was told that nothing was wrong with him. Reliving those lonely, isolated years, self doubt began to plagued him as he questioned his future. One morning as he struggled to open his eyes, Bill said, "Maybe I wasn't supposed to live." My heart sank. Rushing to the phone, I called a dear friend that gave me the number of a fine psychologist. Even though it was our first conversation, she cleared her schedule and saw my Bill the following morning.

This excellent therapist helped move my son beyond depression and low self-esteem. While resolving his past, she guided him in putting the pieces of his life back together. Within a few weeks, Jim and I saw a remarkable change.

Even though Bill never played the violin again, after a few months of therapy, he took an interest in the trumpet. He joined his school's marching band. He became active in the drama department and even sang a few solos in the productions of "Godspell" and "You're A Good Man Charlie Brown." Choral singing, history, political science and debate emerged as his passions.

Bill graduated from high school in June 2003. His acceptance at Messiah College in Grantham, Pennsylvania begins a fresh new chapter in his life. His expectancy and determination will help me to let go and say goodbye. He is a young man who has a deep abiding faith in Jesus Christ.

No longer do I need to fear leaving Bill alone. (If I say it enough, I'll begin to believe it!) He has had three years to learn how to live with Addison's Disease and properly medicate himself when his body fails him. Fatigue and body aches do plague him during stressful times. His immune system is compromised. Therefore, he does get ill quite often. But adequate sleep, proper diet and exercise have helped to thwart off prolonged recoveries.

Three incidents landed Bill in the hospital during his high school years. Two stomach viruses brought us to the emergency room. After Bill was placed on an IV drip of hydrocortisol, fluids and anti-nausea medications for six hours, any threat of a crisis was avoided. When Bill faced necessary surgical extractions of his wisdom teeth, he was hospitalized for three days in order to avoid any possibility of another Addisonian crisis. The planning of this surgery was approached with great care by his endocrinologist and his oral surgeon.

Initially after his hospitalizations, I panicked as I thought of Bill moving 80 miles away from home to attend college. I had been his advocate for so many years. Who would be there for him? Yet I now give thanks to God for allowing these situations to arise while Bill was still in high school. We've been able to devise a plan that would come into effect in his Dad's and my absence. His treatment is no longer met with uncertainty, for now his illness has a name.

He has Addison's Disease, and his future remains in God's hands.

Bill knows that his miraculous healing is for a greater purpose in service to his King. Our family watches with grateful anticipation as Bill fulfills his dreams for his future, obtainable dreams given to him by his Lord.

I thank our Lord, Jesus Christ for this life and the next. For eternity is only a breath away.

Joel 2:25
"I will repay you for the years the locusts have eaten."

BOOK II

Essays of Love

Table of Contents

1	A Job To Do	
	Kim Ketchum	183
2	In The Warmth of the Son	
	Jan Maloney	189
3	The Gift	
	Jim Maloney	193
4	Protecting Amanda	
	Susan Zych	199
5	His Word; Our Obedience	
	Dottie Schaefer	205
6	She Needs A Name	
	Ken Tucker	211
7	Perfect	
	Colette McGuire	219
8	Strength Beyond Measure	
	The Gresalfi Family	225
9	"What's Wrong Officer?"	
	Ginger Gibson	233
10	"A Burp Cloth? You've Got To Be Kidding?"	
	Kim Lewis	239
11	Grace	
	Jackie Stevens	245
12	Once Again, It's Time To Pray	
	Sharleen Dluzak	251
Epilogue	Isaiah 60:20	
	Karen Rhea	257

Author's Note

I believe most profound people can communicate effectively with very few words. Yet when we express our children's encounters with suffering, it is very difficult to encapsulate our journeys. Most of my interviews resulted in the opening of wounded hearts and raw memories. Every child in this book represents thousands of similar encounters. That is why the following stories are so dear to me.

Therefore, sit back and open your heart. And if you choose, read an appropriate essay out loud to someone who could use a word of encouragement or a bit of sobering perspective in their own life.

1

A Job To Do

1

A Job To Do

Kim Ketchum

Wesley was dying. My little boy was only 24 hours old, yet his future drew bleaker by the hour. My limited time at home was consumed with tearing the house apart, trying to find a music box. I knew we owned one. The nurses in the pediatric ICU said that music would be very therapeutic for my critically ill baby. It was the only task that made me feel as though I had a part in his comfort. Tears welled up in my eyes as my hand grasped the stuffed musical lamb. I had to get it back to the hospital. Now Wesley would soon hear the melody that would soothe his fragile body.

The previous day, my husband Steve and I listened to Wesley's gasping breath as he was momentarily placed in my arms after an endless labor. He was whisked away within seconds. We knew something was amiss. Two years earlier I savored precious time with my first son, Steven, following his uneventful delivery. No, something was terribly wrong. Initially the doctors minimized Wesley's breathing difficulties, stating that a breathing tube had been inserted into his airway. Yet in the middle of the night he was airlifted by helicopter to Children's Hospital. That morning I was released from the maternity ward, and Steve took me directly to Children's to see my new born son. Upon arrival, we called our family and close friends to let them know of Wesley's deteriorating condition.

Strange how people react in a crisis. Family members that we would ordinarily depend on couldn't handle the stress at the Pediatric Intensive Care Unit. If I dared to mention the possibilities, even the most supportive family and friends changed the subject. I felt as if I were losing my mind. The one person that showed great compassion was a neighbor who went to church. She listened to everything I told her. Her job, she proclaimed, was to get Wesley on a "prayer chain." She said she would also call her church and neighbors, asking everyone to pray for our little boy. She was a great comfort to me.

Yet nothing could have prepared Steve and me for the assault on our senses at the PICU. I watched helplessly as Wesley was put on a paralytic drug. Every function in his tiny body was being taken care of artificially. He had a condition called pneumothorax. Forced oxygen had caused multiple pin size holes to be blown through his lungs. The doctors called it a freak of nature. His blood gases showed very little oxygen. Large incisions invaded both sides of his little chest. Protruding breathing tubes from the incisions sustained his life. Wesley's condition was grave. I listened to several doctors bombard us with medical terminology. Their approach was no nonsense and blunt. Six other infants and their parents were in the PICU. One other baby had the same condition as Wesley. How could they both appear so beautiful as their lives hung in a delicate balance between life and death? The mood was somber, for what could we possibly say to each other? There were very few pleasantries exchanged, for who would go home to an empty nursery?

Late Saturday night we arrived home to cards, flowers and a huge blue stork in our front yard. It stated Wesley; 8lbs. 4oz. But he wasn't with us. As I drifted off to sleep, I thought of our neighbor that was praying for our family. We were awakened in the middle of the night with a phone call from the hospital. Wesley was not going to make it. Steve and I raced the 40 miles back to the hospital to be met by a doctor that explained our only option. The ECMO was an iron-lung type machine. It could save his life, but the possibility of long term disabilities were discussed. The machine would cut his main artery, bypassing the lungs. Steve and I went home to make our decision. I shuttered to think that our son's life could depend on us speaking the words "Yes" or "No." It was early Sunday morning; hence we titled that grievous day, Black Sunday.

That very morning, Wesley amazed everyone. We were spared any decision of his treatment. Wesley began to show signs of remarkable improvement. The medication to paralyze him was stopped. As his ventilator was removed, he began breathing on his own. Feeding by mouth was a problem, as the initiation of the sucking instinct had been missed. Yet eight days later, Wesley was breast feeding, and fourteen days later he was home. His progress was watched closely for eighteen months. We were assured that his childhood would be unaffected by the critical, first two weeks of his life.

Looking back, our inappropriate dubbing of Black Sunday was actually the day when the prayers of many summoned all of heaven, and the Lord healed Wesley on the Sabbath. I know there was a miracle on that day. I thank

God for a neighbor who had a job to do.

Romans 15:5
"We each have different work to do. So we belong to each other, and each needs all the others."

2

In The Warmth of the Son

2

In The Warmth of the Son
By: Jan Malony

⚘

It was the winter of 1996. We had already spent 45 days at Children's Hospital in Washington, D.C. (Ten more days were to come.) Daniel had gone through the worst of it already; two and a half weeks on a respirator, followed by three surgeries on one day; a tracheotomy, a gastro tube placement and a three inch slice of muscle taken from his thigh for genetic studies.

My husband and I had fallen into the rhythm we had adopted so many times before. Each of us took turns spending the night at Daniel's bedside, while the other replenished with a good night's sleep at home. I spent my days with my son, for a special needs child requires so much more care than the nursing staff has time to give.

But today was the day that I lost it. I just could not do it one more hour. It was the first time I cried and the emotion poured out in torrents. That cold morning, I rushed out of the hospital, having been there through the night, trusting Daniel's care to the nurses. They already had the daily seizures and insulin-dependent diabetes to deal with, besides the current events.

I drove the fifty minutes out to the suburbs where we lived. I went through the drive-thru at a fast food chain and bought a soothing, warm cup of coffee and equally warm muffin. I drank and ate. The warmth of the food and the heat of the bright winter sun pouring through the windows, enveloped me like a blanket. I reclined my seat and fell asleep for several hours. Peace and tranquility covered me and I literally felt God's arms, delivering me from all the pain, worry and endless fatigue of the past weeks. He cradled me and I was renewed.

I would once again have the strength to be Daniel's mom.

Isaiah 40:31
"but those who hope in the Lord will renew their strength. They will soar on wings like eagles; they will run and not grow weary, they will walk and not be faint.

3

The Gift

3

The Gift
By: Jim Malony

I really don't remember if it was snowing, because the windows at Children's Hospital were so dirty that only the brilliant illumination of the Capitol dome, two miles away, was vaguely discernable on the quiet, lonely Christmas Eve. It was very late, maybe near midnight. The hallway lights had been dimmed and the swing-shift had settled into its routine.

Dan's breathing had improved, so for a change we found ourselves out of the pediatric ICU and alone in a two-bed room. Instead of Christmas tree lights, we had the twinkle of modern medical technology. The monitors, IV pumps and the other accouterments of very sick kids blinked and flashed in the darkened room.

Christmas in a pediatric hospital is at once touching and at the same time, oddly funny. Well meaning community groups bring gifts and goodies, so the kids see Santa maybe six or eight times over the course of a week. Black Santas, white Santas, fat, skinny, old, young, male and female Santas. And here in Washington D.C., we have the First Lady's annual "photo op" with a group of sick children who have no idea of who the dear woman is. Don't get me wrong: we moms and dads are grateful, if not just a bit amused at this holiday-induced spasm of good cheer.

But this night—this lonely, dark night—was to be briefly different. The family had long since left. Dan's mom and big sister were now safe at home, and I sat in his hospital room reading. At first I only heard a few notes; the seemingly random tinkle of piano keys somewhere in the night. A while later the sound grew louder and more recognized with the unmistakable strains of an often sung Christmas carol. Soon, down the hall came a man in a tuxedo, pushing the hospital's old upright piano. He was a local lounge singer, a piano-bar guy who any other night of the year would be entertaining patrons at a local watering hole. His broad smile and dogged determination to get that old piano down the hall, told me that here was the true spirit of Christmas. For here was a solitary man, humbly giving himself to others without expecting anything in return.

He poked his head in the door and asked if I had any request. He smiled at my choice and played a few bars of the old sacred hymn. Then he wished me a merry Christmas and pushed on to the next room, while I pondered this small act of kindness from one stranger to another in the middle of the night.

"Silent night, holy night, all is calm, all is bright..."

Psalm 63, 5-8
My soul will be satisfied as with the richest of foods; with singing lips my mouth will praise you. On my bed I remember you; I

think of you through the watches of the night. Because you are my help, I sing in the shadow of your wings. My soul clings to you; your right hand upholds me.

4

Protecting Amanda

4

Protecting Amanda

Susan Zych

Amanda was five years old when her physician diagnosed her with asthma. I didn't know whether to be elated or grieved. Rarely affected by symptoms during the day, each evening was a grim reminder of countless nights gone by. The coughing, wheezing and gagging were as predictable as roosters crowing at dawn. Nightly, my husband David and I would put our heads on our pillows and close our eyes. As we would just begin to doze off to sleep, we would hear a tiny cough, then another, then another. After 45 minutes, Amanda would appear in our room, asking for my help. After administering her medication, I'd lay down with her, waiting for her symptoms to subside. Now and then we'd try hot steam in the bathroom, or I'd pound her back, trying to help her move the phlegm. The routine left me weary. Yet in the quiet hours I would pray for my daughter and our family.

Each morning, as the sun streamed through the window, I had to often stop and think, "Am I in my own bed with David or is this Amanda's room?" I was left sleep deprived, wondering how this was affecting my younger daughter Emily. The undercurrent of stress and fatigue was only apparent when David and I were alone. Caring for my chronically ill daughter left me with very little energy in tending to my husband and Emily.

Above all else, I hated how this illness affected Amanda's social life. Once Amanda returned from a sleep over at a friend's house and announced, "All the girls are mad at me because my coughing kept them awake." From that time on, I always gave other moms a heads up, letting them know I was just a phone call away. I hated to rob her of opportunities that other little girls experienced, such as slumber parties and camping with the Girl Scouts. So I became the leader for my daughter's troop.

One evening, on our troop's first sleep-out, there were seven tents pitched in my back yard. As the chatter of excited little girls slowly subsided, Amanda's coughing began chirping in chorus with the crickets. The protective mama bear in me kicked in, as I snuck her in the house to cough the night away. I managed to save her from the ridicule of the girls. At 5:00 a.m., I slipped her back in her sleeping bag, as I quietly went in my tent. One hour later, everyone began to stir. The conversation centered around preparing breakfast. The girls were unaware that Amanda had been indoors all night.

Amanda's asthma began to subside during her adolescence. I don't remember when I began to sleep with David each night. It just happened. I do know that it was in high school that Amanda began to refuse her medication, explaining that her heart would race after she used the inhaler. Yes, she did grow out of her asthma.

Driving with Amanda from Poolesville, Maryland, to Seattle, Washington, to begin her master's program, we reminisced. She looked at me blankly as I talked about the years of sleepless nights during her childhood. She had no recollection of those endless evenings of coughing and gagging. God truly did enable me to do a pretty good job of protecting her. The memories were mine alone.

"Lord, thank you for your protection and provision during my little girl's childhood. I also thank you Father, for being there for David and Emily, quieting each of us with your love."

Jude 20
But you, dear friends, build yourselves up in your most holy faith and pray in the Holy Spirit.

5

His Word; Our Obedience

5

His Word; Our Obedience
Dottie Schaefer

Mark had my full attention. In the middle of his sentence he paused. It was a disturbing pause. My husband Dave and I called it "Mark's blockage." With the sweetest intentions, his little brothers would fill in the missing word. Quickly rescued, Mark would stop stumbling over the letters K, D, L, or T before getting back on track to complete his sentence. Very bright, he often found an appropriate substitute word when stuck for an uncomfortable length of time. Dave and I knew that Mark needed professional help. Our little boy was only four years old.

He seemed to stutter more frequently when under pressure. Very large for his age, adults often expected far more from Mark than was age appropriate. Topping off the pressure, he was a people pleaser. He took to heart every request and every rejection. When elementary school began, the demands of performance increased. Unfortunately, so did Mark's stuttering. He was an excellent student, but when forced to read out loud, he stammered repeatedly. In the 1960's, few public school teachers were educated in the field of speech impediments.

A viable option was to take him to the Easter Seal's Treatment Center. For unknown reasons, a full year of speech therapy was not helping him. Their recommendation was to terminate his therapy and have his doctor prescribe a muscle relaxant. So we complied. Poor Mark. Only six years old, and the more we tried to help him, the more he felt something was wrong with him. He hated therapy and he hated the medication. We could not bear to discontinue seeking help. There had to be treatment available for his stuttering. It broke our hearts to witness Mark getting worse, not better.

The following year, Dave heard a local radio station advertise a foundation in Harrisburg, Pennsylvania that specialized in speech impediments and therapy. Hopeful, we made an appointment for Mark. But Mark did not want to miss school and was quite upset that he had to go to another doctor. Distraught, his stuttering increased. Yet what choice did we have? The medication was not solving Mark's problem, and possible help was only two hours away.

The night before the appointment, our three boys were asleep. Dave was sitting on the sofa in the living room, reading his Bible silently. I sat beside him and read over his shoulder. The words from Psalm 118: 8 jumped off the page. Interrupting my husband's quiet meditation, I asked if he had read verse 8. Sure enough, at that exact moment, he also read it. There were four columns of scripture and the Holy Spirit revealed His word to us, simultaneously! *"It is better to take refuge in the Lord, than to trust in man."* Awe struck, Dave and I discussed the possibility that we were putting too much trust in therapists and doctors. Was God trying to tell us something? We got down on our knees and asked the Lord to guide us in our decisions regarding Mark. After praying, we knew we would cancel our appointment in Pennsylvania the next morning.

Mark seemed so relieved when a typical school day preempted another doctor's appointment. A trip to Pennsylvania was never to be. Several days later, Mark asked why he wasn't taking his medicine anymore. His Dad picked up the bottle of medication and threw it in the trash, saying, "You no longer need it." Nothing else was said. There was no doubt that Mark was tiring of the search for man-made solutions.

What a relief to witness our son's remarkable progress. Not to say that there wasn't an occasional blockage in his speech. But we agreed that God would receive all the glory for Mark's improvement. Dave and I lost all concern for Mark's speech impediment. We were thankful to God for His healing hand, and we continued to trust His Word. We believed that our faithfulness would be imparted to Mark.

In high school, the evidence of Mark's dependence on God's grace was revealed to us. Strong and aggressive, he was asked to be a captain on his high school football team. My concern surfaced. How would he call the plays without stuttering? With adrenaline pumping and teammates awaiting his calls, this was a recipe for disaster. Committing his speech to prayer before every game, Mark never failed to communicate clearly. His high school won the Maryland State Championship in 1976. Mark started the first Fellowship of Christian Athletics at Seneca Valley High School. Our son's speech impediment was being used to draw him to a closer relationship with Jesus.

After receiving his masters degree in civil engineering from The Pennsylvania State University, Mark was hired by Bechtel Corporation upon graduation. Early on in his employment, he was assigned to a project in Houston,

Texas. Mark was asked to return to Maryland and speak in front of Bechtel's executives on his accomplishments for the Houston project; the exact situation Mark dreaded. The telephone rang. Mark was very nervous and pleaded, "Mom, if I ever needed prayer, I need it now." After explaining the demands of the upcoming speech that evening, I assured him that his dad and I would pray, just as we had many times before. Hours later, Mark called us, clear and articulate. His speech went off without a hitch.

God revealed His Word to us 37 years ago in the quiet moments in our living room. Our refuge and obedience remain in Jesus Christ. Without a doubt, Mark is a faithful man. He is now imparting that same reliance on God to his son, Eli.

Acts 5:29
"Peter and the other apostles replied; "We must obey God rather than man."

6

"She Needs A Name"

6

She Needs A Name

Ken Tucker

※

"Ken, you're not going to believe this; my water just broke." Karen's word's cut like a knife. I will never forget the tone of resignation and sadness in my wife's eyes. At only 24 weeks pregnant, our baby was given a twenty percent chance of survival. We had arrived at the University of Maryland Medical Center less than 24 hours earlier to try and stop Karen's premature labor. The medication had failed. In the middle of the night our daughter was born. Because she was a girl, her survival rate was raised to forty percent. She came out screaming, so we knew she was a fighter.

The hours after her birth were pure agony. We couldn't get any information. Not knowing the condition of our little girl was brutal. I was instructed to stay by Karen's side. Torn, I naturally wanted to be with Karen, but I felt an urgency to see my daughter. Every hour I would leave the room to go in search of information. Over and over again I returned without news. Karen and I made a decision that our little girl would not leave this world without a name. Jillian Grace Tucker would appear on her birth certificate and her tombstone. As dawn streamed through the hospital window on that February morning, my daughter's prognosis was revealed. She weighed 1 lb. 11 oz. Her stomach was not developed. A respirator and full oxygen were sustaining her life. Jillian was so fragile that we were not permitted to touch her. But she was alive.

I saw her first. She was so premature that her skin was transparent. Every vein was visible. She had no skin coloring. Her eyes were sealed shut. I couldn't decide if she resembled a new born puppy without hair or if she appeared alien-like. Her appearance was frightening to me. After sterilizing my hands, I reached into her isolette. As I placed my hand next to her, accenting her tiny form, Jillian's first finger and thumb grasped my hand. Instantly, I fell in love with my daughter.

The doctors didn't pull any punches. Because of Jillian's early arrival and her necessity for full oxygen, there was a high probability of brain damage, blindness, deafness, cerebral palsy and multiple handicaps, if she lived. The testing was endless. I cringed with every IV needle stuck in her tiny body. Yet I was compelled to stay by her side.

A full month went by before Karen and I introduced our daughters, Caroline, 5, and Morgan, 4, to their critically ill sister. The girls would draw countless pictures of angels to place in her isolette. The nurses never threw any of them away. They became layered on the wall behind her. Various sized stuffed angels, even bear-angels surrounded Jillian. It was as though love was wrapped all around her. This aspect in the neonatal ICU was comforting. Everything else in our lives was hard.

Our family's routine was to drive 45 miles from our home in Frederick, Maryland to the NICU in Baltimore every Saturday. We would attempt to take the girls for outings to the Baltimore Aquarium or the Inner Harbor to add a bit of diversion. In their eyes, Jillian was getting all of our time. Our lives became a juggling act. During the week, Karen would drop the girls off at daycare and drive to Baltimore to spend the day with our sick baby. I would drive an hour from home to my office in Washington, D.C. Late afternoon, Karen would go home to be with Caroline and Morgan. After work I'd hop in the car, driving another hour to the hospital. There I'd sit with Jillian and form precious relationships with the night nurses. Karen and I would often compare notes on our daughter's progress at midnight, only to awake the next morning and repeat the routine of many weeks gone by. My contact with Caroline and Morgan for four months was spent on the cell phone after leaving work.

One evening as I drove north to Baltimore, Karen put Caroline on the phone. She burst into tears and asked me to come home. My heart sunk when she pleaded with me, "Please don't go to the hospital!" After I explained that her sister was very sick and needed either mom or me by her side, there was silence. Caroline said, "I'm feeling sick too, daddy." I told her that I would do whatever she needed me to do. When I gave her the choice, Caroline gave me permission to go to Jillian. We were all under the strain of caring for the newest member of our family.

I never spoke of the rawness of my emotions at the time, but I found it strange that no one asked how I was doing. The doctors would address Karen with news of Jillian's condition. Family and friends would ask how Karen and the girls were holding up. The absence of concern for my ability to cope during this time only accentuated the pressure of needing to be strong for my family. I often looked at other dads in the hospital and wondered if they felt equally alone.

Jillian had been in the neonatal ICU for two months when she developed a disease that unless controlled quickly would permanently affect her nerves. She was running a very high fever. It lasted a couple of days before one of the night nurses seemed very concerned. She said the doctors were fearing the worst. When I left the hospital that night, I dreaded seeing Karen and telling her the news. What was to become of Jillian? I called out to God during that hour ride home to Frederick. I recited the Lord's Prayer. "Our Father who art in heaven, hollowed be thy name. Thy kingdom come..." I couldn't remember it. I started over again. "...hollowed be thy name..." What was wrong with me? I had said the Lord's Prayer a thousand times. I tried over and over, but I finally gave up. It was at that moment I cried out to the Lord, telling him everything. "Please, Father, I need you to take care of my family. Please take care of Jillian." I continued my heartfelt conversation with my Father in heaven. "Please Jesus, I need to know that you are with us. I will raise my girls in the church." It wasn't a bargain. It was a promise. Suddenly I was able to complete my prayer.

Entering our home, I found Karen sitting in the nursery. A peace overcame me. Jillian would either come home with me or go home with Him.

The next day Jillian improved. Never again did she face issues based on her survival. Many serious hurdles were laid to rest. She came home after four months in the NICU, diagnosed with cerebral palsy. She wore a heart monitor for eight months. Now and then the alarm would sound. We would shake her, reminding her to breathe. At eighteen months and tons of stimulation by her big sisters proved effective. Though developmentally delayed for two years, she never showed signs of cerebral palsy. At four years old, Jillian is nothing shy of a miracle child.

Looking back at the night when I forgot how to recite the Lord's Prayer, I truly moved to a deeper relationship with the Lord. My Savior met me in the car that night, hearing and responding to a very personal plea from this broken hearted man. He gave me more than I asked for. My family was restored. We are part of a community of faith. And yes, he gave me Jillian.

1 Peter 5:10
"And the God of all grace, who called you to his eternal glory in Christ, after you have suffered a little while, will himself restore you and make you strong, firm and steadfast.

7

Perfect

7

Perfect
Colette McGuire

My life was perfect. "It's a boy," the doctor announced. My husband Scott, yes, my high school sweetheart and I had a little boy to bring home to his two older sisters. Cameron looked like a perfect, ten and a half-pound baby boy. Perfect, except his two big toes looked odd. Pointing this out to the doctors in the hospital, they agreed that his toes had a strange appearance. They seemed a bit perplexed but were not overly concerned. So neither was I, until they told us that Cameron had pneumonia. His delivery was so quick that his lungs took in some fluid and produced an infection. He would have to remain in the neo-natal unit for a week. Hopefully it would clear up. After one week in the neo-natal unit, he was much better, and we had our sweet homecoming with our little girls, Megan and Caitlin.

I was consumed the following three months with a

crying baby. Colic was the diagnosis. Cameron had another unusual trait that we couldn't ignore. His spine had lumps and his back seemed crooked. Surprisingly the x-rays showed nothing abnormal. Scott and I accepted the physician's 'normal' report and watched our little boy develop amazingly well. The crying stopped. Cameron was bright as a whip. Every milestone was timely, if not advanced. He smiled, laughed and ate well. He turned over, sat up and crawled. He walked at nine months old. He brought great joy to our family.

Yet the lumps were always on his back; changing shapes and locations periodically. His toes were still odd. Deep down we knew there was something terribly wrong. When he was nine months old, we finally asked our pediatrician to refer us to the University of Michigan Children's Hospital. New x-rays and further testing by our new pediatrician confirmed that Cameron, our sweet baby boy had Fibrodysplasia Ossificans Progressiva, FOP. I learned that this rare genetic disorder would slowly turn all the soft tissue in his body to bone. He would eventually become one solid piece of bone. The prognosis was devastating: No cure. Any trauma would result in bone growth in that area of his body. One characteristic of FOP was a missing joint in the big toe. The natural progression would affect his neck; he wouldn't be able to look down. Next, the shoulders; lifting his arms would be impossible. Finally his arms, spine, hips and knees would turn to solid bone and eventually his jaw.

My throat tightened. I couldn't swallow. I did not want to break down. We were both horrified. How could this be happening? I wanted to be strong. My perfect life and Cameron's life had just shattered into tiny pieces. Every question that we asked the doctor evoked a response that took my breath away. I had to get home and call our family. Next I called my friend, Linda, my mentor in Christ. I needed to hear her voice, her advice and prayer. Linda said that my life, my fun and perfect life that I had previously known, would now be a journey, seeking His perfect will.

The day of Cameron's diagnosis, a passage of the Bible kept going through my mind. I got out of bed very early in the morning after a sleepless night. Sitting down, I looked up a passage in Romans, remembering that it spoke of suffering. The apostle wrote:

> *"...through whom we have gained access by faith into this grace in which we now stand. And we rejoice in the hope of the glory of God. Not only so, but we also rejoice in our sufferings, because we know that suffering produces perseverance; perseverance, character; and character, hope. And hope does not disappoint us, because God has poured out his love into our hearts by the Holy Spirit, whom he has given us."*

When Cameron grows up, he wants to be an astronaut. Not unlike other nine year old boys, I recently heard him praying for lots and lots of candy. I pray that both of our prayers are a *sweet*, fragrant offering before His throne.

> **"Lord Jesus, I pray that everyone could feel the contentment I feel, knowing you are in control of all things. I ask that you give your wisdom and resources as The Great Physician to the dedicated group of doctors doing research of FOP at the University of Pennsylvania. I pray for a cure, but if it does not come in Cameron's lifetime, I know that he will live with you, Jesus, in a perfect body."**

8

Strength Beyond Measure

8

Strength Beyond Measure
The Gresalfi Family

※

Romantic movies, checking her email and shopping add relaxation to Kristen's busy life. Her smile is radiant, recalling her latest outing with her dad. "We have special permission from The Department of Park and Planning to ride in our golf cart to the lake behind our house and see the dragon flies and thistle!" Laughing, she adds that her dad puts his arm around her shoulder so she won't fall out of the cart. For Kristen is dependent on her family and her wheelchair because of spastic, cerebral palsy.

Born at 29 weeks gestation, Kristen and her twin sister Michelle shared a rough start and their birth date, February 24th. Their parents, Debbie and Michael Gresalfi, were residing in Tucson, Arizona, when the girls were born. Debbie was a teacher, and Michael was in the military.

Tiny, Kristen only weighed two pounds, nine ounces.

Respiratory problems, severe reflux, orthopedic issues and muscle contractures would define little Kristen's early years. She would endure many surgeries before she was four years old. Each physician's approach to her diagnosis was unsettling. One would say very little, while another would present the worst case scenario.

Debbie explained, "Kristen was not going to be the child I envisioned her to be while still in the womb." There were grievous time periods associated with that sobering realization. Raising twins is both exhilarating and exhausting. Adding the daily demands of the extensive physical therapy left Debbie weary. Also the comparisons of twins is to be expected, though Michelle's progress and Kristen's delays brought a myriad of daily emotions.

When Kristen turned four, she began asking her mommy, "When am I going to walk?" She watched her sister skip and run, believing her time was around the corner. Her repeated question broke Debbie's heart. It was hard to believe the extent of Kristen's mobility was about to be determined. Her petite stature enabled Debbie and Michael to easily manage their daughter's physical needs. Riding in her stroller, she looked more like a two year old. She delighted passersby with her infectious smile. But the months had turned into years, as Debbie attempted to protect Kristen from the usual standoffish reaction people have to a person in a wheelchair.

Yet it was Kristen's doctor who called her mother to task over relinquishing the baby stroller for a wheelchair. He firmly explained that Debbie was holding her daughter back with her social skills and hampering her independence. Reluctantly, Kristen's parents put aside their fears and followed her doctor's advice.

Not long after her chair arrived, Kristen and Michelle could be seen racing on the sidewalk in front of their home: Michelle on her bike and Kristen in her wheelchair! The spark in Kristen that was so evident as a baby was about to soar. Even though her childhood would be interrupted with numerous surgeries, Kristen's parents believed their daughter's love of life and learning would overcome many difficult situations. Debbie's personal experience with Kristen gave her a compassionate wisdom that sometimes appeared lacking in therapy and education. Therefore, she pursued her Master's in Special Education. She and Michael did everything possible to facilitate Kristen's independence and education.

When Kristen was eight years old, the Gresalfis built a home in Boyds, Maryland. Michael designed their house to accommodate Kristen's wheelchair. Every bump could be a potential obstacle, so thresholds were absent throughout the house. This was one of several accommodations he insisted on for his daughter. Her motorized wheelchair freely sailed from room to room.

Academics presented hurdles that were not so easily remedied. Note-taking was impossible for Kristen. With great fortitude, she used her two index fingers to type. Turning pages of a book was a challenge, as well. Book stands graduated to e-books and computer discs. Never shying away from difficult school activities, Kristen overcame these obstacles. Fellow students in an academic bind would come to Kristen for tutoring.

At home, she was dependent on her mom for dressing and all of her personal needs. After a rod was placed in her back for sclerosis, she was not able to turn over in bed. Terribly uncomfortable, she would sweetly call for someone's help, asking for a push, enabling her to fall back asleep. Most would have ranted and raved in frustration, dealing with daily pain and dependence on others. Yet her gentle spirit was always evident to everyone.

Kristen's grandmother, Betty, recalls the ripple of joy that Kristen's life has had on others. A small company made

Kristen a beach buggy, enabling family members to maneuver her over the sand at the shore. Years later when purchasing an additional tire for Kristen's buggy, the staff enthusiastically asked about her granddaughter. With great pride they recalled designing and building her buggy. It was quite a challenge, just as everyone in Kristen's life is challenged to recognize the long, hard road of every one of her tiny accomplishments. The rewards, just in her trying, is enough. Betty said, "It enriches everyone who becomes aware of this section of society that was possibly never visited before."

One of Kristen's many accomplishments was completing high school with a 3.76 grade point average. Her bedroom walls display her countless accomplishments and awards that were bestowed upon her. Teacher and counselors wrote glowing college recommendations and shared accolades. They described Kristen as conscientious, intent on independence, funny, smart, full of personal integrity, compassionate, intellectually curious and original in her thinking.

It was no surprise that Kristen would attend college. Confined to a wheelchair, with limited use of her arms and hands, she moved into the dorm at Edinboro University of Pennsylvania. She was delighted as she approached her first year at school. This was not her first time away from home. She had been to summer camps for disabled children during previous summers and loved the experience.

Like many freshman students, Kristen became homesick. She had to arrange for students in her classes to help with her note-taking. The results were not always adequate. Even more distressing, people Kristen was dependent on for her personal needs were not always available. She asked the Lord for His strength and comfort, as she had many times before. In desperation during her first semester away, Kristen called home in tears, begging her mom and dad to bring her home. She believed that going home would be the solution for her stressful situation. But her parents didn't budge. They reminded her that there wouldn't be anything to do at their house. Also, college is what she had worked so hard for all those years. Naturally when they hung up the phone, Kristen's sobs ripped their hearts out. Although they knew Kristen would become a stronger woman for her diligence.

During Christmas break, Kristen came home to enjoy time with her parents, Michelle and her younger sister, Nicole. Returning to her dormitory was now familiar territory. Following her final exams in May, Kristen returned home with gained insight from the previous year. "I feel so blessed for the parents that God gave me." Kristen added that her parents were always there for her, but they were firm. She felt she was never treated differently than Michelle or Nicole. Had it been any other way, Kristen would have never known the gratification of completing her freshman year at Edinboro with a 3.37 grade point average.

2 Chronicles 15:7
"Be strong and do not give up, for your work will be rewarded."

9

"What's Wrong, Officer?"

9

"What's Wrong, Officer?"
By: Ginger Gibson

∞

The brilliance of the blue October sky filled the room where I was adding the final touches to the miniature houses I was painting for my next door neighbor. It was such a perfect day; I looked forward to getting outside. I put the finished houses on a tray and headed next door. A police car pulled up and parked in front of our house. I assumed he was looking for a specific address, so I approached his car.

Stepping out of his vehicle, he introduced himself. "I'm Officer Jones," he said in a calm voice. "Are you Mark's mother?" I froze, but managed to ask, "What's wrong?" The words he spoke left me stunned. "Your son has been in a serious accident and is in the hospital." I asked if he was dead. "Oh no, no," Officer Jones assured me. "He's not dead, but it is a very serious accident. I'll take you to the hospital."

In that brief moment the structure of my life was shattered. I called my husband, who wasn't available, then my minister, then friends in my prayer chain, asking them to pray for Mark. I was told later, by a witness at the accident, that as soon as she saw Mark on the ground, turning blue, she started to pray for him. On the way to the hospital, sirens roaring, I alternately prayed and gleaned details of the accident. Mark had pulled out of the college exit into the path of a large truck. The impact ejected him from the car. A doctor in the building across the street heard the accident, ran out, saw Mark, and began administering oxygen as they waited for the helicopter. "Helicopter," I repeated as Officer Jones told me. "That means it's really serious." "Oh yes," the officer said in his still calm voice.

As my daughter, my minister, my husband and I sat in the waiting room waiting for Mark to come out of surgery, a verse from Isaiah slipped into my mind; *"Fear not, for I am with you."* Somehow, in that anxiety ridden room, I felt a peace steal over me. When the neurosurgeon came out to say that Mark had survived the surgery, I felt a great sense of relief, but not surprise.

In the days to follow, waiting for Mark to come out of his coma, then enduring another surgery to remove a lung abscess, the prayers and support of friends was a great encouragement. At the suggestion of one of the nurses, I began keeping a journal of Mark's day to day progress. Some days it seemed like regress.

Mark was in the hospital for nearly a month before he was transferred to a rehabilitation hospitalization in Pennsylvania. He begged to spend one night at home before we took him to the facility. He lay in the parlor, unable to walk upstairs, surrounded by his beloved cats and dog, family hovering closely.

November drifted into December. A friend brought Thanksgiving treats for all the patients on Mark's ward, and the family celebrated this holiday at the hospital.

Even though Mark thought he was recovering just fine, the doctors felt he had a long way to go. The brain stem injury caused Mark to evaluate things differently. He wasn't willing to look at the whole recovery process. He just wanted to get out. It became his fervent goal to be home by Christmas. We thought we would bring Christmas to him and brought up a small lighted tree and cards and cookies. But he was determined, and I believe, finally wore the doctors down. On Christmas Eve day we brought Mark home to stay. He has continued to make progress and to recognize some of the limitations placed upon him by the brain injury. Presently he has a full time job as night manager in a service station, has health insurance, and rents an apartment. His great love and greatest skill is drawing. He has decided he wants to go back to school to study animation.

> **"Dear God, thank you for your sustaining nurture and guidance. As Mark struggles to find his next step, let him feel your love for him, which has been so evident to me."**

Isaiah 41:10
> *"Fear not, for I am with you, be not dismayed, for I am your God; I will strengthen you, I will help you, I will uphold you with my victorious right hand."*

10

"A Burp Cloth? You've Got To Be Kidding?"

10

"A Burp Cloth? You've Got To Be Kidding?"
Kim Lewis

∞

I never felt clean. The stench of Mason's vomit always seemed to permeate my clothes, my husband's suits, and our home and our car. Being a pastor's wife, I couldn't help but be conscious of my appearance and hygiene, especially during our hours at church. I knew that nasty sour smell could put off the sweetest parishioners. Large cloths were the only suitable substitutes for the cute little decorated burp cloths. Mason actually had adorable clothes, but I don't believe anyone saw his outfits. He was always covered, anticipating his next explosion.

That first year was hard. Countless Sunday mornings began with the best intentions to be on time. Yet inevitably after breakfast, Mason would vomit all over everything in sight, setting me back another fifteen minutes to clean up the mess. When my daughter Morgan was born seven years earlier, I rarely recalled feelings of fatigue and sadness. Our family was seldom late. But Mason's illness added a terribly difficult dimension into our once routine lives. Each day I watched helplessly as my little boy struggled to keep down his feedings. It consumed all of us.

One Sunday morning I was just turning the corner on my post-partum blues. I was finally able to wear a dress that didn't make me feel frumpy. Another sleepless night was not going to get the best of me! In church my husband, Tracy, waved goodbye, as he prepared for his ministry. Entering the sanctuary, with Mason still in his car seat, he suddenly vomited all over his hair, his face and his clothes. I snapped. In despair, I shoved him back in his car seat on the pew. Everything went into slow motion, as I saw his little head slam back against the seat. Startled, he cried out. I silently thanked God that the fear of the moment was his only injury. Guilt welled up in my heart. In tears, I dashed out of the sanctuary in search of my best friend, leaving Mason with his big sister. My friend in Christ consoled me, knowing exactly what I needed. The past months flooded out in detail, as she helped me to clean up physically and emotionally, once again.

Mason was only two days old when I noticed him choking, gagging and spitting up when I'd lay him down after nursing. This was by no means little sputters of breast milk gurgling out of the corners of his mouth. No, vomit would spew in every direction. Acid Reflux Disease immediately came to mind, as my sister's child suffered with this very condition. After Mason's two week checkup, he never kept down a feeding. I began to notice that his little arms and legs would thrash in rapid succession, just prior to vomiting after nursing. I knew he was in pain.

Frantic, I returned to the pediatrician when he was one month old. Yes, Acid Reflux Disease was Mason's diagnosis. Now he would be more prone to esophageal cancer if left untreated. I was instructed how to embark on a two hour ordeal of pumping my breast and adding cereal to his bottle for every feeding. The cereal weighed the milk down, helping the formula to stay in his stomach. Along with medications, adding cereal to his diet would help to alleviate the burning in his esophagus. His lips were too weak to suck an adequate amount of milk, so I bought multiple nipples with different size openings to help provide the nourishment Mason needed. Yet too much milk and cereal flowing through the nipple would cause him to gag, regurgitating everything in his stomach. Projectile vomiting took on a whole new meaning.

    I was instructed to put Mason on his back to sleep. But this seemed dangerous to me. When he would vomit, it would fill up his mouth and block any air through his nasal passages. I used a plastic suction bulb to help clear his nose. I was afraid to leave his side. When my daughter was three months old, the transition of moving her from our bed to her own crib was effortless. In contrast, having Mason anywhere but by my side was pure agony for me. His baby monitor kept me up all night, as his breathing was loud and had an unnerving gurgling rumble. When he slept by my side, I would actually rest for short periods of time. No one in my home was getting my undivided attention. I was constantly sleep deprived.

    At one year old, medication seemed to help Mason keep down his food. Unlike other less fortunate Acid Reflux babies, Mason never lost weight. Unfortunately a disturbing behavior developed after his mealtime. He would appear to hyperventilate, breathing deeply and rapidly. One day it suddenly dawned on me why Mason wasn't getting sick. It was not the medication retarding the vomit. To my horror I realized that the appearance of hyperventilating was the vomit rising from his tiny stomach. He would follow this action with a huge gulp. He had learned to swallow what was being regurgitated. An upper G.I. proved that he still had Acid Reflux. This meant that his esophagus was continuing to be irritated, leaving Mason vulnerable to serious health conditions. Recurrent infections landed Mason in surgery to have his adenoids removed. The acidity from the reflux had repeatedly splashed on the adenoids. The once hard adenoids were now squishy and useless. I cringed at the internal damage occurring because of the disease.

A web site for Gastroesophageal Reflux Disease was a godsend. The ability to network with parents of Acid Reflux children helped me to remember I wasn't alone. Practical advice ranged from new medications to various nipple manufacturers. I needed contact with other parents who would understand.

At two years old, Mason knows when his tummy is full. By not overeating, his symptoms have lessened dramatically. He's a big boy with an infectious smile. Medication and the ability to communicate with his daddy and me have helped tremendously. I want to believe and trust that Mason will one day know the healing touch of Jesus.

Romans 12:12
Be joyful in hope, patient in affliction, faithful in prayer.

11

Grace

11

Grace

Jackie Stevens

Billy suffered with an intestinal disorder. He could not digest his food properly; therefore, he had terrible abdominal pain. His prognosis was not encouraging. By the time he was eight years old, his doctor ordered a bone-age test and concluded that he had the bone-age of a four year old. I was one worried mom, desperate for the healing touch of God. How I prayed for my little boy.

A friend approached me and invited our family to a concert in Bridgeport, Connecticut. A Christian artist named Grace would offer music for our worship and entertainment. Her program would include an altar call and a healing service. Frankly, the music sounded like a great evening out for our family. I was skeptical of Billy being healed through a singer, for I knew how faithfully I had prayed over the years for my son's intestinal condition. I believed that my prayers as a mother were certainly as effective as hers. Setting my apprehensions aside, I decided to go with my family and enjoy the concert by Grace.

The night of the concert my husband, Bill, and I got Billy and our young daughter, Betsy, ready for a fun night of Christian music. Looking at Billy, I knew there was one problem that I should have dealt with that very day. He had a terrible case of poison ivy which had spread beyond the help of calamine lotion. His face was swollen, and it was spreading very near to his eyes. I would have to call his pediatrician in the morning, for medical attention couldn't wait another day. Yet that evening we were all excited to get out of the house and see Amazing Grace, as she was billed on her program.

As I had hoped, the music was uplifting for adults and kids too. An invitation was given for anyone to stand who had a desire to know Jesus as their Lord and Savior. Many did. The Spirit of God was truly present. Grace then asked for anyone who desired healing to come forward. My earlier apprehension faded. Grabbing Billy's hand, I dared to hope. The concert concluded, and as we headed out into the summer evening, somebody said, "Look at Billy, his poison ivy is gone." And it was.

I knew that Billy had received a healing from the Lord. Evidently it was not the specific one I had been praying for, but there was no doubt that my son had received a touch from the Master's hand. In one evening, I was given a visible confirmation that if I continued to hunger for God, He could answer a mother's prayer and a singer's prayer in one fell swoop, for His glory.

For a little more than a year, Billy would continue to suffer. But miraculous joys were around the corner. His debilitating condition went away. The bleak prognosis of stunted growth was proven wrong. My precious, undeveloped boy, has turned into a healthy, six foot tall man.

Hebrews 4:16
Let us then approach the throne of grace with confidence, so that we may receive mercy and find grace to help us in our time of need.

12

"Once Again, It's Time To Pray."

12

"Once Again, It's Time To Pray."
Sharleen Dluzak

Mark came down with the usual childhood disease, chicken pox. Rather than a trip to the drug store for calamine lotion to relieve the itching, my husband Rick and I headed back to the National Institutes of Health (NIH) in Bethesda, Maryland, our home away from home. Mark's rare genetic blood disease, Wiskott-Aldrich Syndrome, had proved fatal to all of the boys who inherited this disease. Mark shared Wiscott with his younger brother, Matthew. Few had lived past the age of two. The boys were now in grade school. They had made it this far, yet now a common childhood disease was threatening Mark's life. A Wiscott child had never survived chicken pox. The word went out to family and friends around the country: "Pray for Mark."

As Mark's body fell prey to the onslaught of chicken

pox, his devastating symptoms raged. Every square inch of his body was covered in pox sores. I could not place the tip of my finger on any part of Mark's skin that was not covered by a pox mark. He started slipping into a coma, for the pox were now internal. Transferred to intensive care, we sat vigil by Mark's bedside. I meditated on Proverbs 3:5: *Trust in the Lord with all your heart and lean not on your own understanding.* I pleaded, "Lord, he's only eight years old; he's just a little boy. Please don't take him; let him live. You've brought him so far."

I recalled the numerous hospitalizations through Mark and Matt's young lives. Colds turned into pneumonia. An eye infection caused a detached retina. High fevers, paralyzation, ear infections, swollen glands, bruising, bleeding, surgeries, transfusions, infections and croup kept the boys in the hospital. We were there so often that our family became well acquainted with the nurses and doctors and they knew the boys.

Reminiscing in the confines of my heart, I remembered conceiving after numerous heartbreaking, failed treatments for infertility. Our disappointments turned to joy with Mark's birth. But it didn't take long to realize something was wrong with my baby. Mark was fifteen months old and I was five months pregnant with Matt when Mark was diagnosed with Wiscott. My dream of a large family was fading. As I pondered our family's future, my obstetrician felt that my ability to conceive again was virtually impossible.

So imagine my surprise a few years later when a sonogram showed that I was once again pregnant. This time, it was twins. Due to bleeding, I was admitted to NIH on full bed rest. Rick and I hardly knew anyone in Maryland. In the confines of my hospital room, my mind whirled as I tried to arrange child care for my boys. All of our extended family lived in California. We were in a real dilemma. Rick had to work, for our medical bills prior to NIH were astronomical.

So we managed the best we could.

At 5:00 a.m., Rick gathered up the boys to visit me at the NIH. Mark was four and Matt was two. They climbed in bed with me, as Mark turned on the television. A few minutes later a nurse walked in my room. In a panicked search, her eyes began darting back and forth, asking where the boy's father was. I explained that he left for work. Color drained from her face. "What? This is not acceptable!" Telling her our predicament, I announced, "I have a plan." Someone would take the boys from 9:00 a.m. to 4:00 p.m. to the NIH playroom. This supervised facility was provided for admitted children only. Yet Mark and Matt had played there many times during their own hospital stays. They would join me for lunch in my hospital room. I assured her that Rick would take them home when he got off work. She was speechless, knowing this was the only option for our family. Our plan worked.

Research on Wiskott-Aldrich Syndrome had shown that a successful bone marrow match was the boys' best chance for survival. The twins were fraternal. My mind whirled with excitement. I saw this as a great miracle. I said to God, "I see your plan Lord; one twin's bone marrow will match Matt and one will match Mark and we'll live happily ever after!"

On July 20, 1977, David and James were born. They weighed a tad over two pounds. The bone marrow transplants were never to be. David lived seven hours. James lived two.

I snapped back from my past grief to Mark's present crisis. A doctor walked into the room to discuss his deteriorating condition. He felt Mark's only hope for recovery was an experimental drug that had never been previously used. His life was terribly fragile, and we were ready to try anything. They began the medication. All we could do was watch and wait. Soon the pox started fading.

Mark was the first Wiscott child to ever survive chicken pox. Matthew was the second.

Rick and I petitioned God with our prayers and our faith in Jesus Christ. After years of medical setbacks, as well as undeniable miracles, Mark was called home to be with Jesus when he was 15 1/2. Matt lived another three years. We were given 13 additional years of loving our sons than the doctors had ever imagined possible.

There are times when my grief is raw. Missing my boys and reliving their trials can consume me certain times of the year. Yet joyous, very personal moments with Mark and Matt fill me with precious memories. I praise God for His word and the assurance of an eternal perspective. One day we will hear the words, "Mommy and Daddy" again when we come before our Redeemer and see our four boys, sitting at the feet of Jesus.

Epilogue

Isaiah 60:20
Your sun will never set again, and your moon will wane no more; the Lord will be your everlasting light, and your days of sorrow will end.

Bear with me as I explain why I ended "Sick Kids" with Sharleen Dluzak's terribly sad story. I always knew the final essay in this book would be hers. The sobering reality of life is that not all of our children live to adulthood. I am so honored to say that Shar is a dear, personal friend. As she and her husband loved our family through the years of Billy's illness, their presence was greatly anticipated, but terribly unsettling at the same time. I often wondered, "What if the Lord has brought Shar and Rick into our lives to prepare us for the worst?"

On the contrary, The Dluzaks sat by our son's bedside in the ICU, insisting that we get a bite to eat in the hospital cafeteria. Jim and I broke down as we wondered how they could bring themselves to come to the pediatric ICU. Their minds and hearts must have been filled with grief as they sat by Billy's bedside, thinking of their own teenage boys' countless hospitalizations. I know they prayed for our son's life and rejoiced in his recovery. Yet as Billy's spared life allowed us countless celebrations of birthdays, holidays and even his high school graduation, Shar and Rick will never experience the joys we have been granted.

Sadly, I never knew Matt and Mark. All I know is that their mom is an incredible woman. Rather than curling up in a ball and closing the door of her heart, she nurtured me into absolute healing. Shar and Rick have served countless broken-hearted people. They facilitate the grief ministry at our church.

Shar reminded me that we are never to minimize our grief and pain or compare our loss with someone else. It makes her very uncomfortable to have someone say, "Oh this is nothing compared to what you went through." Instead, she encourages everyone to keep their eyes on the Lord, identifying with Him in His suffering, not hers. I believe a part of Shar must have died with each of her boys. But there is a scripture verse that fully explains how she goes on.

Galatians 2:20
I have been crucified with Christ and I no longer live, but Christ lives in me. The life I live in the body, I live by faith in the Son of God who loved me and gave himself for me.

I want to thank Jesus Christ for providing me with a praying family and a body of believers that helped me in maintaining a grip of assurance in a world that seemed to be slipping through my fingers. Because He first loved me, by forgiving my sins on the cross at Calvary, I was able to give Him my anger and grief. Only then was I able to actually give thanks for every soul who fell short in my son's life.

For in their weaknesses and human imperfections, my Savior's mighty hand was revealed. He truly is The Great Physician.

In the Precious Name of Jesus Christ,
Karen Rhea